Behind the Scenes
The True Face of the Fake Faith Healers

by

Yves Brault

DORRANCE PUBLISHING CO., INC.
PITTSBURGH, PENNSYLVANIA 15222

The following publishers have given permission to
use quotations from copyrighted works:
From *The Wizard from Vienna*, by Vincent Buranelli.
Copyright © 1975 by Vincent Buranelli.
Reprinted by permission of McIntosh and Otis, Inc.
From *The Edge of Disaster*, by Michael Richardson.
Copyright © 1987 by Michael Richardson.
Reprinted by permission of St. Martin's Press Incorporated.
From *Franz Anton Mesmer: Between God and Devil*, by James Wyckoff.
Copyright © 1975 by James Wyckoff.
Reprinted by permission of John Hawkins & Associates, Inc.

ISBN # 0-8059-4069-3

Printed in the United States of America

First Printing

For information or to order additional books, please write:
Dorrance Publishing Co., Inc.
643 Smithfield Street
Pittsburgh, Pennsylvania 15222
U.S.A.

Beware of false prophets, who
come to you in sheep's clothing,
but inwardly they are ravenous wolves.
You will know them by their fruits.
Matthew 7:15-16

DEDICATION

This book is dedicated to all those women, children, and men who have suffered spiritually, physically, and emotionally because they were manipulated and exploited by fake faith healers, preachers like Benny Hinn and his peers. To all those sacrificed lambs, we express our compassion and our love. This book may not heal all their wounds; nevertheless, it exemplifies that somebody cares enough for them to disclose what many had to go through.

Contents

ACKNOWLEDGMENTS

I need to thank my wife Nicole, our daughter Melanie, and our son Stephan for their ideas, their constant support, their patience, and their understanding.

Foreword

This book relates a true story that corroborates one more time the axiom which states: truth is stranger than fiction.

This unadulterated story abounds with tears, sorrows, deceptions, seductions, lies, and corruptions.

It exposes the true face, the mesmeric practices that faith healers use under the name of God; individuals who are sheltered and shrouded with a specious presence of zeal which comes from their own pride, malice, covetousness, greed, and ambition.

It is also a story filled with love and trust among and between the members of my family; my wife Nicole; our daughter Melanie; our son Stephan; and myself, Yves, the happy husband and father.

Most of all, it expresses the strong unity in my family that helped us live through all the tribulations, the ordeals, the sufferings, and the hurts that would have most likely destroyed a lonesome heart.

CHAPTER ONE
SHEEP VS. WOLVES

It felt like being hit by a two-ton truck.

I went flying out of the Judge Macgill Theatre, landing on the red-carpeted floor of the Robson Square Conference Centre.

What happened? Had all the forces of hell struck me?

When I got my senses back, my wife Nicole was trying to refrain a man from hitting her; then my son Stephan ran to his mother's rescue, but a security guard and his supervisor quickly grabbed him. These peacekeepers seemed more interested in helping the attacker than in protecting an innocent lady. A representative of the Robson Square Conference Centre also rushed to the scene but only to tie Nicole's hands behind her back leaving her totally defenseless in the situation. Things happened so rapidly that Melanie just froze watching the whole scene.

What in the world was going on?

It is the price Peter Popoff's ministry had us pay for interfering in one of his so-called Miracle Services in the city of Vancouver.

I need to narrate the facts that caused such a physical demonstration of "Christian brotherhood" that evening.

I had perused some material about Peter Popoff and his ministry in the Vancouver Public Library. From it I learned of his exposure on *The Tonight Show*—a national disclosure that took place in 1986. The investigation of the methods utilized by Peter Popoff to deliver accurate "words of knowledge" in his "Miracle Services" led to the discovery of a plot between his wife and him. He would receive from his wife, via a hidden receiver in his ear, information from inquirer's prayer forms or cards which he would use while ministering to the audience. I had never seen him on television, nor had I attended one of his meetings.

After being exposed on national television, Popoff altered the name of his ministry. He dropped the name Peter Popoff Evangelical Association and selected the name, People United For Christ. They must carry their own definition for unity, for the altercation on that Monday night simply does not comply with their new name. Without a doubt there was not too much harmony that evening. Nevertheless it showed their real colors, their true face. The name has been changed, but their nature remains.

So allow me to explain how that episode took place. On Saturday, November 26, 1994, I read in the weekend edition of The *Vancouver Sun* that Peter Popoff and his ministry were in town. They held two single meetings: one on November 28, the second on the 29th at the Robson Square Conference Centre.

Despite our knowledge of his fraudulent methods of manipulation, all the family decided to go to his Monday night meeting in order to check him out, to observe his ways of operating. We had been deceived by so many ministries in the past that we wanted to see for ourselves how this one functioned.

We arrived on the premises around 6:45 P.M. and were greeted by Pastor Paul Collett who, as Popoff himself told the crowd later, had been involved with Popoff's ministry for many years.

The service started around 7:00 P.M. We could not count more than thirty people in the room at that time. Pastor Collett spoke first. He said so many beautiful things concerning the burden Popoff had for the Russian people. He said that Popoff loves them so much that, as a matter of fact, he had on his heart to solicit, especially for them, a special offering. This offering of just five dollars would be used to forward Bibles into Russia. "You can give less than five dollars if you want," Collett told the crowd.

It is really amazing that these guys always have burdens for people remotely located!

The people were asked to bring their offering to the front and drop them in a basket that Pastor Collett was holding, naturally. What a good way to monitor the crowd and to verify if anyone suffered from a physical disability! These guys surely know where their bread and butter are. They did not get a single penny from us. We would certainly not encourage such a fraud.

After the offering Collett introduced Popoff and we were asked to stand, applaud, and give honor to whom honor was due. This act of humility really touched my heart! Then Popoff repeatedly had us sit, stand, raise our arms, and even wave for Jesus. Our actions were supposedly to praise, thank, and worship God. The five-minute workout was rather a scrutinized analysis to detect the people's obvious physical disorders.

Popoff predicated for about twenty minutes; afterwards he decided to walk the aisles so he could lay hands on people. As Popoff explained, God would give him words of knowledge concerning illnesses, diseases, or physical disorders for certain spectators. Then he would lay hands on them and pray for their complete healing. Strangely enough, "words of knowledge" came out only for those who had obvious physical problems or for those who had given at the offering.

So he started to walk the aisles and to lay hands on people. The first one he went to was an elderly gentleman who had helped them earlier in the service by distributing prayer request forms.

These prayer request forms are very peculiar. On one side, you are invited by Brother Popoff to write anything that is on your heart, like a need that you might have, or maybe just something you would like to share with him. Then you write your name, address, and at the bottom you check one of the lines that corresponds to the amount of offering you intend to give. On the flip side you come across a statement that reads:

> I, The undersigned, hereby give consent to People United For Christ, its agents and representatives and, waive all rights for the use of my name, picture, and any statements made and testimonials given by me in any manner it deems useful.... I further, hold harmless, People United For Christ, its agents and representatives from all liability or claim regarding all activity associated with the meeting in this city on this date.[1]

And then you are asked to date and to sign. No member of my family filled out the form or signed it. We really wanted to see if Popoff could reveal anything to us without referring to some information recorded on the given form. Of course, anyone who signs that statement has no legal recourse against Popoff or his ministry. These guys act very cautiously.

So Popoff asked the elderly man, "What's wrong with your shoulder, brother?"

The man answered that he could not lift his arm. Popoff asked the man to lift up his two arms so he could pray for a complete recovery. The fact that his whole left arm—not just his left shoulder—was handicapped appeared obvious to us. The crowd had just to look, they could plainly see the problem.

Popoff, however, tried to hide this fact. Not only was his diagnosis wrong, but he never dared to admit it. So he also laid his hands on the man and claimed a total cure for his shoulder.

The poor man's condition had not improved. He was unable to easily lift his left arm. Yet Popoff told the gentleman to praise the Lord and kept on pretending the man was healed. He walked further up the aisle, stopped, and pointed out a lady.

He addressed her, "There is something wrong with your left side?"

The lady bluntly answered him, "No."

So he swiftly passed her by. He kept on walking the same aisle ignoring us. No wonder! We did not participate in the offering, nor did we have any evident physical disorder.

Then he asked a lady sitting behind us, "Is there something wrong with your left side?"

Again he received a negative answer.

He asked a third lady. It seemed the left side of the body obsessed Popoff.

She said, "No, it is my right side."

Popoff insisted that the pain was on the left side.

The lady kept on saying the pain affected her right side.

Finally he prayed for a complete healing. And as if it were a common habit of his, he asked the lady if he could shake her a little bit. Upon the agreement, he then took hold of the lady's head and shook her. Must I say that his manners and the tone of his voice expressed a lot of aggressiveness.

We had ourselves been deceived by so many charlatans that we just could not endure seeing these true, honest, and credulous people being lured and tricked by that so-called "man of God," whose only goal was to demonstrate a superior ability of healing in order to gain the people's confidence and money.

At this point several people left the room. Just outside, in the lobby, comments of disapproval were shared. With another man that deprecated him, we decided to walk back in and ask Popoff in a very polite manner if there was any truth in the literature criticizing him, and if any truth resided in the facts exposed on national television. And also, if the facts were true—and they really were—why then he would not apologize to all the many true and honest people he had tricked in the past by fetching money from them.

Popoff did not dare to answer the questions.

So we asked him again.

Still no answer.

The man who accompanied us really became insistent. You could tell that Popoff felt very uneasy. Being asked before a crowd, composed of a certain proportion of his followers, to comment on affairs that he attempted to avoid really perturbed him.

We asked him one last time, but instead of answering us, he addressed the audience enjoining them to pray because he claimed we were sent by the devil to disrupt his meeting!

Three or four minutes elapsed before we decided to walk out. People here and there interrogated us about the whole matter. No one from Popoff's organization advised a member of the family to leave the premises; although few people around disliked our insistence.

Feeling the situation was becoming chaotic, we decided to leave. On my way out of the auditorium, near the door, a young man questioned me in relation to God and the reality of healings. I had just started to answer him when I got hit in the back by Pastor Paul Collett—the two-ton truck!

During the altercation a man called the police. Unfortunately, they arrived on the scene after the whole wrangle was over. The officer took the version of the security guards, then ours, and he advised us to go home.

The following day, on November 29, I called the Vancouver Police Department to get a copy of the report on the incident #94/320123. The officer, however, told me that I could not get a copy because I was only a citizen, and that they are solely given to lawyers or insurance companies. In spite of his refusal, I asked the officer if he could read it to me. He agreed. Amazingly the name of the "two-ton truck" did not appear on the report!

Would you believe that the security company hired by the Robson Square Conference Centre saw us and others in the crowd as agitators? And that they did not intervene against Popoff's man because he was part of the ministry who had paid for renting the room? This bold declaration was mistakenly unveiled by Mr. Herb Ainsworth, the superintendent of the security company.

We were told that on the second night less than fifteen people attended Popoff's meeting, and that the management had reinforced the security. As a matter of fact, there might have been more security guards than spectators.

It is sad that people prefer supporting large evangelical organizations, or well-known televangelists, because they falsely think that the bigger, the better. As a result, opportunist ministers elevate themselves to the shaky pedestal of fame, power, and influence in order to better build their empire.

Those individuals pretend to have a burden for distant places where they are ministering to the masses, but chances are that you do not have the resources or information to objectively verify their stories. Yet, they do not even care for the person standing feet or even inches from them!

Why am I writing this book?

To inform those dear people who have been robbed emotionally, morally, and financially by such charlatans; and to warn others that could, otherwise, fall into their very seductive enticements. Those dear people are the reasons for this book.

CHAPTER TWO
ON ROAD TO CALVARY

Let me narrate how our adventures began. It all started in 1991. It was proposed, while visiting some friends in Montreal, to view a videocassette of faith healer Benny Hinn.

Nowadays Benny Hinn is probably the fastest rising star in the polluted firmament of the televangelists in the United States. He is seen and heard daily on several of the Christian television and radio networks in the United States, Canada, and around the world.

All these television and radio broadcasts plus all the books he writes, and the audio and videocassettes he sells are merged under Benny Hinn Media Ministries. They later added the name Benny Hinn Ministries. He also pastors, with the help of a staff of about twelve men, the Orlando Christian Center—commonly called OCC—but later rebaptized World Outreach Center. I wonder why! Is Benny acquainted with Popoff's way of management?

It is a church that welcomes every Sunday approximately seven thousand devoted fans. His headquarters are located in Orlando, Florida.

Benny and his crusade staff also hold "Miracle Crusades" on a monthly basis all over the United States. He also travels around the world for various events and special projects.

This couple, friends of ours, were partners of his ministry. This partnership meant that they were committed to send every month a certain amount of money. Such donations are employed to keep the ministry on the air. Those donations originate from all classes of society and amount to millions of dollars annually. Most of it is utilized to buy broadcasting time, as well as generous salaries, opulent homes, and expensive benefits for the preacher.

In return for their tax-free donations, partners receive each month a videocassette of the latest Benny Hinn miracle healing service, or one of his teachings, or one of his books, or even a coffee mug. This is a common way to operate in the Christian television circuit. Partners with their monthly pledges are the spinal cord of TV broadcasting.

Our friends usually go on vacation in Florida once a year. They had seen Benny on the Trinity Broadcasting Network, were seduced by his mesmeric power, and then later decided to become partners.

So that evening, for the first time, we watched a videotape of Benny Hinn's "Healing Service."

At first sight we were not impressed.

Why?

Because Benny was touching people left and right, and almost every one of them was ungracefully falling down. It seemed bizarre that God was using such a procedure.

Too many things happened that we had never seen before. We were quite skeptical.

Perhaps we should have kept our first thought. On the other hand, if we had stuck to it, we would have never discovered the real face and techniques of mesmerism; this book would never have been written; and you would have possibly never heard about the hidden side of those "beautiful" ministries.

A short while after this visit and the discovery of the "great man" Benny Hinn, my boss told me he had a condominium to rent for the holiday season. He said that he preferred renting it to me. We agreed on the terms and all the family was on the way to spend Christmas 1991 in Ponce Inlet—a suburb of Daytona Beach, Florida. Daytona Beach is about an hour's drive from Orlando.

Before our departure, a friend suggested that we should visit two churches in Orlando. The first one was called Resurrection Life Center, where Willie Hinn is senior pastor; the second was called Orlando Christian Center (OCC), led by Benny Hinn. Yes, they are brothers. We intended to visit one church and possibly visit both of them.

So we departed Montreal by automobile Friday, December 20, 1991, and arrived at our destination late Saturday night.

Our condo was just across the street from the ocean. The weather was great, the ocean waves were warm enough at least for us "snowbirds," the shopping prices were quite affordable. This vacation promised to be refreshing.

On Sunday night we decided to go to Orlando in order to find either Willie or Benny Hinn's church. We looked all around town to find Willie Hinn's church, but we could not locate it. So we decided to look for Benny's. A police officer helped us, and we arrived at OCC around 8:00 P.M., nearly two hours after the beginning of the service.

Despite the rarity of empty seats, one of the ushers found some room for us way in the back. By the time we got seated the special Christmas carol service was almost over. The whole ambience of the church was impressive and its people were very friendly, so we elected to go back to OCC for the Christmas Eve service the following Tuesday night.

So on Christmas Eve we arrived an hour and a half before the service and were greeted by an usher, a very sweet man. When we mentioned to him that we were visiting from Montreal, he went and talked to the head usher. The lady responsible for the front row seating came to us and offered us a seat in the fourth row. We naturally agreed.

I must say that the greeters and the ushers of the church were very kind and polite, even though they have to work under a constant stress caused by the volatile temper of Benny. In general, you can feel that ushers care for people.

We were very satisfied with our visit at the church and unanimously decided to return the following Sunday for the morning services. The first one starts at 8:00, the second around 10:30.

Like our previous visit, the praise and worship led by pastor Jim Cernero was great, and the preaching by Pastor Benny Hinn was flamboyant. Benny has to live up to his image.

He mentioned during the service that he had made a promise to God. The agreement was that he would never ask the congregation for money or for special offerings for the ministry. He said that God had showed him that he should produce and sell videos of his teachings and crusades; and in return, God would provide sufficient funds by the sales of these same videos. Such a statement impressed us, to say the least. This minister seemed to come from a different breed than the usual televangelists who constantly ask for money.

As you will ascertain later, he broke the promise he made to God. In fact, Benny Hinn is a person who very seldom keeps his word.

We stayed in Orlando that Sunday in order to attend the 6:00 P.M. service. Again we were blessed by the praise and worship and by the preaching. After the service we drove back to the condominium.

We spent our leisure time in Daytona Beach bathing, shopping, relaxing, enjoying life, and in all things thanking God for His blessings.

The next service at OCC was to take place on New Year's Eve at 7:00 P.M. We were not going to miss it.

Again we got there ahead of time. That gave us a chance to browse in the church lobby and bookstore and also to chat with people in the church. We had the chance to converse with the lady responsible for the book table. We had been told that Benny had a very busy schedule, so we asked her if he would be present for the service.

She seemed very surprised by our question, but promptly answered, "Pastor Benny is always in church. He never misses a service. You can be sure that he will be here." Later, however, the trend changed a lot because the frequency of his absences increased dramatically.

That New Year's Eve night the church had three special guests: Steve Brock, Alvin Slaughter, and Ron Kenoly. These three gentlemen are among the best male vocalists in the Christian world. Benny had decided to broadcast his service live, via satellite, across the nation. It was a spectacular moment. Benny always goes "first class," as he says. The show really impressed us.

Very strange things happened that night. After the songs, the praise and worship, and all the excitement, Benny started using his "anointing." For those who are not familiar with the process, Benny uses his "anointing" to touch people, and when they are touched, they fall on the floor under the "power of God."

Let me be honest with you: we also fell down like many others. The mystical atmosphere had prepared us, and we had accepted the erroneous doctrine that if you fall down, you automatically receive some spiritual blessings. If you submit your mind and body to that sort of manipulation you will experience these effects. This was our first encounter with mesmerism.

One gentleman got hit by that "power" and remained motionless for at least two hours. He was really stunned. The guy sat there on the platform, lying on one of the pastor's chairs, petrified like a statue. He did not even blink an eye. The ushers had to carry him back to his seat.

After that exhibition of "power," Benny said that God had talked to him and gave him a clear insight of events that were going to happen in 1992.

According to Benny, God had revealed to him that Fidel Castro would die in the middle of the year—1992—and that Castro's death, of course, would mean the end of communism in Cuba. As the year passed by his version changed! Benny later said that Castro would die in the middle of the 1990s. The Bible, however, says that when the word of a prophet comes to pass, that prophet will be known as one whom the Lord has truly sent.[1]

The "great man" Benny Hinn also ridiculed some of his pastors who did not attend the service because they were on vacation. He boastfully mentioned on stage, "I never take vacations. I don't need them, and don't believe in them." Is it not astonishing that a married man with children does not see the evident necessity for a family to take a vacation at least once a year? Later, however, he also changed his mind on this point.

That same night he gave his own highly priced diamond ring to Pastor Bill Byrd, one member of the OCC pastoral staff.

Bill Byrd held the position of principal at the OCC Academy, the expensive private school of the church. He was fired some months later. Things and situations change very quickly in the universe of Orlando Christian Center. The administration of the church even had the security guards of the church escort Bill out of the school! They ordered him to leave the premises *tout de suite.*

Shortly after his departure, the church officials—in their usual way of not giving the congregation a decent explanation on how and why Bill Byrd was leaving—gave him a check of $10,000 to help him open a new church. An act of love? No, a good bribe!

Nevertheless, after that amazing New Year's Eve service we were thrilled. Melanie said to God in the course of the service, "If it is your will, bring us back to this church."

The firm message in her heart sounded as clear as this, "You will be back here sooner than you think." We thought that we would be back in July—for our next vacation. Things, however, were going to be quite different.

During our vacation we attended six services at OCC, and each time we had reserved seats in the third or fourth row. This is quite an exploit. You will find out why later.

We left Ponce Inlet on January 2, 1992.

On our way back to Montreal, each of us carried the hope in our heart that we would go back to Orlando. Events in OCC had been so unusual and so filled with excitement that we were convinced that God dwelt in their midst. We had never been in a church of that size, counting so many members, and with such great music; for all of us, it merely represented the spiritual experience of our lives.

Nicole, Melanie, and I all worked full-time for the same pharmaceutical company. Naturally, we had many keepsakes to share with our fellow workers. Stephan was completing his Bachelor's degree and had already started working on an important engineering project. He also shared our experiences with his friends.

And each member of our family prayed every day for God's direction and for His will concerning His plan for us, especially concerning Orlando. In our spirits and hearts we felt more and more the strong conviction to move there.

Shortly after, one morning in January, God strongly impressed in my heart and spirit to move to Orlando 120 days from that day. He also revealed to me that Benny Hinn would go to Europe. Then we knew for sure we had to move to Orlando.

This had been a very exceptional time in my life. I do not believe those preachers who pretend they talk with God each and every day of their life. They create the impression of possessing a private phone line to the Father in heaven. It implies that the connection gives the preacher a particular power to manipulate God. They may believe they converse with Him, but there is a world of difference between a monologue and a dialogue.

At dinner I narrated the whole story to my family. They marveled at the answer, and were all excited about the plan.

So acting upon this confirmation we went to the Montreal public library, found the yellow pages of Orlando, and made photocopies of all the information we needed. Stephan and I sent, in our respective fields, more than 150 résumés to different firms in Orlando and its suburbs. We were searching for work and attempting to secure the required working permits.

On a Friday afternoon, February 7, 1992, although I had been working for my company for almost three years as a distribution center supervisor, and despite the fact that he had given me a raise before the Christmas vacations, my boss—the same one who had favored me by renting us his condominium in Ponce Inlet—fired me!

After my dismissal the company started losing sales—as much as half-a-million dollars a month. Consequently Nicole and Melanie, who worked for the same company as I, got laid off in the month of March.

God had started showing His plan. We had to advise our landlord of our early departure because we would leave on May 27. Though our lease didn't expire until the end of June, the new tenants agreed to rent June 1st. The matter was well resolved.

Stephan's final semester at McGill University ended on April 22. We decided to drive to Orlando the following day in order to find a place to rent.

In Orlando our footsteps were also well ordered. Flipping through a tourist booklet I noticed an ad entitled, "Would You Like to Live in the USA?" I immediately dialed the given number and asked for some information. In that year Canadians could apply for a working permit commonly known as a green card. I don't have to describe our excitement. We paid the requested fees amounting to $1,060. Our hopes were running high.

We found a beautiful apartment site located in a gorgeous community. Since we had no credit reference in the States, the management agreed to sign a lease under the condition that we paid in advance. We had savings, so this was not a problem.

During those first few weeks we attended OCC and we made new friends. A couple even invited us for lunch on Mother's Day. What a blessing! It was a real demonstration of hospitality.

We got back to Montreal mid-May. Many things were left to be finalized. The place we rented in Orlando included all the major appliances. Therefore we had to sell ours. We even organized a weekend yard sale which proved to be very successful.

Excitement was the only word that could describe our feelings. Our dream of a lifetime was coming true—we were going to live in the United States.

Some of our closest friends invited us for a farewell dinner. It happened on three occasions. For some it was an au revoir, but for one of our friends it really meant a farewell—because he died of a heart attack five months later.

How do you move a six-room household (including the Christmas decorations) to a city fifteen hundred miles away from your country?

You will soon find out.

CHAPTER THREE
ILLUSIVE DREAMS

To move our furniture from Montreal to Orlando we needed to rent a truck in the United States. We needed a twenty four-foot Ryder truck, and we got one in Plattsburgh, New York. Again the way was paved.

Generally when you rent a truck in the United States, the Canadian customs will not allow you to drive the truck into Canada, load it, and then drive it back into the States without a proper permit because someone could do some illegal trafficking.

I called the Canadian customs and explained our situation to the officer. The lady agreed to let us in and out of Canada but only if we would do it within twenty four hours. We did it exactly the way the customs required.

In Montreal we had another proof of the love and kindness of our friends. Four men from the first church we attended came to help us load our truck. What a blessing! Their help was deeply appreciated.

So the truck was loaded, the farewells were said; even if all the family was tired, we were all full of excitement. Our expectations were at their highest level.

Here we go!

In the Ryder truck sat Stephan—he was the starting driver—and Melanie. Nicole and I sat in our little four-door white Isuzu Stylus automobile; and on the back seat were our dog and our cat. Yes, they were also going to Orlando.

We drove to the Huntingdon, Canada/U.S. border. There we faced our first opposition. The American custom officer had us going through a relentless round of questions. While I tried to answer all of his inquires at the best of my knowledge, Nicole, unfortunately, used the officer's personal restroom. Wow! That really made him resentful.

And to top it all, Melanie, in her anxiety, hit a red button and the emergency alarm system went off. So at about two o'clock in the morning, we had all those sirens blowing, and all those red and yellow spotlights flashing.

The American officer, who was very displeased and upset after these events, called his superior at another border office, this one located in Lacolle-Champlain. After consulting his supervisor the verdict came out, "You are going back to Canada, I am not letting you into the States. You can try the customs in Lacolle-Champlain if you want. Good night."

So we turned around and drove to the Canadian custom office just across the street. A Canadian officer, realizing our awkward situation, promptly said, "Go first into the Canadian custom office in Lacolle-Champlain and have a list of the furniture you are bringing into the United States stamped by a Canadian custom officer." It was a priceless advice.

Now we understood why Melanie had, in the night preceding our departure, been impressed in her heart to make a list of our furniture. In the morning she had announced to all of us the necessity of making such a list. No one had thought about that.

Lacolle is about twenty-five miles east of the Huntingdon border. So here we were, in the middle of the night, driving the two vehicles in the midst of those very narrow country roads, toward Lacolle. During the short trip, each of us felt at perfect peace in our hearts. We knew God wanted us in Orlando.

When we got to the Canadian custom office in Lacolle we stopped and had the list of our furniture stamped. Then we drove further down to the American border. There were a few vehicles in front of us and only one lane open. So we patiently waited our turn.

Amazingly, the American custom officer stopped and examined every vehicle very carefully. He checked every driver's and passenger's identity, and made phone calls on top of that.

Then our turn came. I went first with the car.

The officer asked me three questions.

"Are you Canadian citizens?"

"Yes, we are," I promptly replied.

"Where are you going?" the officer asked.

"Orlando," I answered. "The truck right behind me contains our furniture."

"Do you have a list of your furniture stamped by the Canadian customs?" he asked.

"Yes officer, we do," I answered.

Then he declared, "Well, have a good trip!"

My wife and I could not believe our ears and eyes. What would have happened without that list?

So I pulled aside to wait for Stephan and Melanie riding behind us.

The officer asked the same first question to Stephan. He immediately replied that he was with us, and that he was transporting our furniture.

The officer simply said, "Well, have a good trip!"

We had made it! We were in the United States. We stopped at the first gas station on the highway so we could fill the car's gas tank. As we were gathered next to the truck, two police cars unexpectedly arrived.

The opposition resurfaced.

The two police officers acted very differently. One was nice and polite, the other one had a mean and nasty behavior. The latter tried in various ways to have us say that we came to the States to work illegally. I guess he wondered what a group of people were doing next to a twenty-foot rental truck in the middle of the night.

After some very long minutes of discussion and parley, they decided to let us go and wished us a safe trip.

Driving from Montreal to Orlando, a distance of about fifteen hundred miles, is quite a long ride. We were anxious to arrive but when you drive a truck, and when your pets are riding with you in the car, you can imagine the type of adventure we had. We arrived in Orlando Friday afternoon.

The next day, although we were tired, everybody put in an extra effort to unpack the cartons, set up the bedrooms, and arrange the apartment properly. By Saturday night we had almost everything set in its proper place. We went to bed early because we all longed for the next morning. We were going to church; we were going to OCC.

Needless to say, we arrived in church very early. Each of us dressed very sharply— which is a must when you attend Benny's church. It gave us an occasion to renew friendships, but it also enabled us to get good seats in the church. When twenty-eight hundred people assemble for a church service, you have to be there very early in the morning to beat the crowd.

The service started on time. During the praise and worship, Pastor Benny arrived on stage. He was excited and showed us a letter he had just received. This letter was an invitation for him to go to Europe and to appear on Super Channel—the European television network that broadcasts across the continent to as far as Russia. God had revealed the same thing to me five months earlier, more than fifteen hundred miles away.

As days went by we finished decorating the apartment. It looked charming. Even more we really felt at home in Orlando.

As my wife and I were conversing in French in the lobby after a Wednesday night service in June 1992, a lady came to us. She was overwhelmed because she heard us speaking in French. Her name was Jeannine, but everybody called her Jean. She came from Vermont and spoke French. She said she had prayed for six years to have a French-speaking friend, and she thanked God she had found one.

Her husband Bill Welker was in charge of the Sunday school. Like in all the churches, there was a serious lack of benevolent workers for all the ministries, but particularly for the Sunday school. We felt in our heart that we should go and give them a hand.

So the whole family got involved in the church. Three of us helped in Sunday school: Stephan as a coordinator, Nicole in the snack department, and I worked at the registration desk. Melanie joined the church choir.

For the six months we helped in Sunday school, the children ate Cheerios cereal or Cheez-it crackers, and drank concentrated apple juice diluted in water and ice. So that children could enjoy some variety for breakfast, some Sunday school teachers often brought muffins, cookies, or Crock-Pot slow cookers filled with hot cereals from home.

Many of these children rarely had breakfast at home, and thus depended on the food given during the Sunday school classes. Meanwhile the choir, between the first and second service, was treated to an of all-you-can-eat breakfast with plenty of bagels, cream cheese, coffee, juices, and milk. How revolting, but not surprising! The choir, whether in church or on the road, was a central part of Benny's mesmeric show. This is why he pampered them.

Nonetheless, the worst aspect of the situation was that the school building—just adjacent to the main building—was furnished with some restaurant equipment. For an unknown reason that equipment did not work. Goodwill contributed to the organization and the kitchen could have been put in service efficiently. They could have purchased food at discount price in some supermarkets. One food chain had even offered free items. Only the administration knows why they refused. Perhaps the operation was not evaluated as a good investment.

Jeannine Welker was very well-known in the church. Sure, her husband directed the Sunday school, but she also carried a reputation of her own. Jeannine was a prayer partner. These volunteers pray with people every time the pastor makes an altar call, which happens almost every service.

Her older daughter Michelle babysat Suzanne and Benny Hinn's younger children. Jeannine also bragged that she had a direct line with Benny. She said she could phone him whenever she wanted. That represented an incredible situation for us.

Jeannine had a very interesting side in her personality—she had visions. One of her most famous visions concerned the wedding in two years of her seventeen-year-old daughter Michelle to twenty-eight-year-old Kenny Smith, the personal bodyguard of Benny at the time. She pressured Kenny so much that she almost convinced him to marry her daughter.

As far as I know this wedding has never taken place. A few months later, Kenny Smith was framed and fired by the Administrator, Gene Polino. I will tell you about that later.

We volunteered in Sunday school class for the eight o'clock Sunday service. After the children were given back to their parents, we would go to church where seats were supposedly reserved for the Sunday school staff. Every Sunday, however, we had to struggle to get a seat because the 10:30 A.M. service attracts a larger crowd.

In big churches like Orlando Christian Center, the right to have a good seat turns into a masquerade, a farce. The first three rows should be known as "no poor man's land." They are reserved for the pastors and their wives; for friends of the ministry; for the members of the board; for special guests; and for those who are part of the "in crowd"—by this I mean those who are carefully hand-picked by Benny and/or Administrator Polino.

Most of the time they are wealthy people, sharply dressed and well groomed; but many of them cannot hide their dry and miserable souls. Some church members live so far under the Christian standard that you would have to backslide to be in fellowship with them. Nonetheless, remember that birds of a feather flock together.

Ordinary people have to be in church at least ninety minutes before the service starts to get a decent seat. It upsets them to see that every Sunday, at every service, some members—always the same ones—arrive five minutes before the service or even sometimes in the early part of the service. They then sit at their "reserved" places in "no poor man's land."

There are two kinds of love, two sorts of kindness in Benny's church. The big valley that divides the people is called money and reputation. There is an old saying that goes like this: Such is the pastor, such is the flock.

Those lackeys come to church only to be seen and acknowledged by Pastor Benny, and then they go and tell all their friends about the special treatment from which they "Benny"fit. They do not follow God, they follow a man. The human nature needs to look for idols.

I cannot help suspecting that Jesus, who delighted in the company of the poor, who had supper with whores and tax collectors, and befriended sinners, would treat such crowd with the same mockery. He challenged the religious leaders of His time, accusing them of hypocrisy and of setting forth one rule for the rich and another for the poor.

I do not remember, in all the services we attended at OCC, seeing Suzanne Hinn,

Benny's wife, arrive on time even once for a service. She would walk in, followed by a babysitter carrying one of their two young kids, and march down the aisle of the church five to ten minutes after the service had started. Maybe she did not realize that by arriving so late, she disturbed the whole congregation.

And that, my friend, shows only the tip of the iceberg. Stay with us for you will learn things that will alarm you. You will learn how it really works behind the scenes of that ministry and others.

Next we will discuss the famous anoint"Hinn"g. Of course, we all notice the misspelling of this word. I have intentionally misspelled the word, just like Benny Hinn has intentionally misled his followers that his "anointing" is from God.

CHAPTER FOUR
THE ANOINT"HINN"G

Faith healer Benny Hinn alleges that the Holy Spirit has personally given him an "anointing" to heal the sick. And of course, according to him and his peers, God gives His anointing only to very special people—men and women who have lived incredible spiritual experiences. Their definition of experience includes many visions of Jesus and multiple encounters with the Holy Spirit.

The most interesting part of that gift resides in the fact that Benny Hinn utilizes the "anointing" everywhere and anytime he decides to do so. Benny has reached a point where he firmly believes that he does not follow the Holy Spirit, but that the Holy Spirit follows him! In reality, and it is sad to say, he is led by a devilish spirit.

This book proves that the false anointing practiced by Benny Hinn and other fake faith healers is nothing but *mesmerism* which they use very wisely to control the emotions of the crowds. An emotional and well-planned crowd control disposes, of course, its attendants to hand out bigger offerings and donations.

Those performers want us to believe that they are not in the ministry for money! You can fool one person all the time; you can fool everybody once; but you cannot fool everyone all the time.

Mesmerism, sometimes known as controlled hysteria, is defined as follows: the capacity of raising the emotional state of an individual, or a crowd, to an abnormal, but controllable, intensity. Mesmerism is the forerunner of today's hypnotism.

This type of mind control is exercised in the name of God to usurp lots of money from trustful people. The Scripture says, "My people are destroyed for lack of knowledge" (Hosea 5:6a). How true and accurate this statement is.

Mesmerism originates from Europe, but it reached the United States early in the nineteenth century, where it successfully spread and remained. America received its first full dose from the Frenchman Charles Poyen. A very capable speaker and author of a pamphlet promoting the spirit of Christianity, his fantastic healing methods proliferated throughout the country. Mesmerism and its esoteric practices had entered into the American religious culture.

Preachers like Benny Hinn, on top of possessing an attractive magnetism known as charisma, plus an intangible something which women call charm, but men call strong personality, use that charisma to draw thousands and thousands of people in their deceitful trails. In return, when these people are hooked, they give thousands and thousands of dollars to these ministries.

For many Christians, faith healers command respect because they falsely think they represent contact with some higher order of existence, which they call God or the Holy Spirit. Faith healers also teach their followers that they possess an intensity, an authority, and a dialogue with God. That lie rests in the fact that people accept and trust such sayings that God operates only when asked by "anointed" individuals like Benny Hinn. In other words, you increase your chances of being healed if you let them ask God for you. What a deception!

Their disguised claim of having a place of mediation between God and man is a clever form of control, but remains chiefly a pretext to stay above all criticism.

If we take for granted that the anointing Benny uses comes from the Holy Spirit; then, when he operates under that "anointing" he ought to be filled with the fruit of the Spirit, that is, love, joy, peace, longsuffering, kindness, goodness, faithfulness, gentleness, and self-control (Galatians 5:22-23a).

Well, my friend, get ready for a surprise. If you only rely on what you see on the TV screen or on the stage, I fully understand why you may believe in their subterfuges. I did too. But thank God, I can now figure them out, comprehend, and expose their tactics.

Now let me go back to mesmerism and define its nature, and how faith healers manipulate it.

The verb "to mesmerize" means: to hypnotize; to spellbind. The verb entered the language of the West as a synonym for "to throw into a trance."[1] It is better known today as being "slain in the spirit," or "falling under God's power." Mesmerism was formulated by Franz Anton Mesmer.

Who is Franz Anton Mesmer?

Franz Anton Mesmer was born May 23, 1734, in Iznang, a small German village close to the Swiss border. At the age of nine he entered a school run by Catholic monks where he began the studies that would prepare him for the priesthood. In 1750 Mesmer entered the University of Dillingen, before proceeding on to the University of Ingolstadt, both located in Bavaria. Both universities were institutions ran by Jesuit priests. However, he found that what he really searched for was in the field of medicine. In 1765, after six years at the University of Vienna, Mesmer passed his medical examinations with success. He then began his practice in Vienna.

The inference has been made that while completing his education, Mesmer studied the occult sciences associated particularly with the name of Paracelsus, the reputed magician and medical innovator of the sixteenth century. It has also been assumed that Mesmer had some acquaintance with societies preaching hermetic doctrines and the "wisdom of the East" such as the Rosicrucians and the Freemasons.[2] That Mesmer was a Freemason is almost a certainty. In fact, only one source says that he was not. He also had a lifelong friendship with Mozart, a Freemason. Perhaps this connection strengthened their relationship.[3]

He devoted the thesis of his medical studies to the influence of the planets on the human body. Mesmer suggested that while the planets exert an influence on the human body, human bodies themselves carry a magnetic, curative fluid, or invisible energy which make them have a therapeutic effect on each other.

According to him, an unbalanced supply of that fluid in the body would make the difference between health and illness. Therefore, Mesmer spent a great deal of effort in trying to master that "fluid." He thought that his discovery meant that, when applied upon the human nervous system, it would make him capable of healing a whole range of ailments plaguing humanity.

Franz Anton Mesmer put together ideas like suggestion, autosuggestion, and stroking medicine in a scientific, systematic method, then popularized his concept. Now referred to as mesmerism, it is described as the ability to insert and implant suggestions ranging from a mild intensity to a near total bondage.

Franz Anton Mesmer, considered the architect of modern hypnotism, was not only a physician but also a healer. He performed his healing practices in the same manner faith healers operate their ministries today. Although hypnotic phenomena are as old as humanity, Mesmer made a science of it. We could say that Mesmer discovered controlled hypnotism.[4] Faith healers now exploit it.

The Laying on of Hands

Mesmer exercised the laying on of hands by touching or making passes with his hands close to a body. Mesmer would point his finger at a patient standing sometimes many feet away from him; the next instant, the patient's body would lie on the floor in convulsions.

Here are a few notations made by Mesmer himself of those he cured. These notations could well apply to Benny Hinn and other fakes. Pay a special attention to how Mesmer's patients reacted to his "anointing."

> A paralytic patient: "As soon as I pointed my wand at her left side, Mlle. Belancourt staggered and fell to the floor in violent convulsions."
> A neuralgic patient: "When I pointed my wand at him, this caused him to tremble wildly; his face became flushed; he appeared about to suffocate; he perspired profusely; he fainted and fell back on the sofa unconscious."[5]

During a séance, Mesmer would stand still and fixedly stare into the patient's eyes, make passes with his hands before the face of one person, and ignore another. When he judged the moment right for any patient, he would inject his mesmerism by touching or stroking, or he could simply point at him. Those people would suddenly scream, fall back, and go into convulsions.[6]

Here is what people of his days thought about his technique:

> ...the mesmerizing process was thought to require a special setting removed from the hustle and bustle of daily existence.... The patient was to become silent, self-effacing, and submissive before a healer who was understood to be in special rapport with higher cosmic powers.... It was commonly believed that, while the operator passed his hands over the patient, a "substance emanates from him who magnetizes and is conveyed to the person magnetized by the will."[7]

Benny uses exactly the same technique. Individuals who come on stage are silenced and completely submissive to his commands. He goes from one to another led, he says, by the Holy Spirit. He stares fixedly into the eyes of his victims, lays hands on them, and the next moment they are on the floor. They fall down under, what he calls, "the power of God" while he says things like, "Oh, the power of God is all over you, darling." Then the same phenomena take place: people scream, fall back into a state of semiconsciousness, sometimes going into convulsions and often displaying hysteria.

At one point Benny was even striking people with his suit jacket. He does not do this anymore—it became too controversial for him. Things change after being exposed on national television.

Think about it for a second. If Benny, as he says, was led by the Holy Spirit to strike his admirers with his jacket, it had to be beneficial in some ways for them. And if God really ordered Benny to do so, then why did he stop obeying God? Unless this demonstration of power came from his basket of entertaining tricks.

He uses his "anointing" and people fall under the so-called power of God. Surely, his techniques are not Godlike simply because he uses the name of Jesus, God, or Holy Spirit; or because he claims to be doing the work of God.

Mesmer had come to the conclusion that the passes he made with his hands were the essential part of his art. At the same time, he realized the non-effectiveness of his cure unless the patient fully cooperated with him. It was essential to establish a rapport or the treatment would fail.[8] In fact, the ability of gaining control of the patient's will was crucial to any treatment's success.

It had been and may be called "faith" by some, a term widely used, and I say has been profoundly corrupted in the Christian world through the years; but Mesmer called it rapport. It is unfortunate that so many people are victimized by a growing number of quacks who operate behind a Christian facade.

Vincent Buranelli commented on the séance of Mesmer. He wrote:

> Since Mesmer recognized the part suggestion and imagination play in the healing process and since he understood the influence of the surroundings on both, he took great pains to provide his patients with a setting in which they could be persuaded to submit to his technique. His whole purpose was to establish rapport with them, to gain their confidence and trust, and then, their nerves being now receptive, to introduce doses of…magnetism into their bodies.[9]

Mesmer, in his séance, used the dim lights, the music, and the rest of the paraphernalia as stage properties to set the mood for his patients, not to deceive the gullible.[10]

Benny uses the same routines, not because he wants to help, but because he covets money, glory, and power. No wonder he spends so much effort in providing the best setting for his admirers: the best singers, the best musicians, sometimes a star from Hollywood, or a political personality. He boasts, "Everything must be first class. Christians deserve the best." Hasn't he shown he likes the best for himself?

He also establishes an emotional affinity with his followers. Once Benny has gained their trust by pretending he possesses a unique connection, a conversiveness with God; once he has gained their confidence, he injects his anoint"Hinn"g—mesmeric doses—to his followers that are now completely under his controlling power.

According to Mesmer, convulsions were part of the healing process. Well when you observe a healing service starring Benny Hinn you will notice that the people, who, by the way, run over one another to be touched by the "great man," have the same reactions: convulsions, fall backs, shakings.

Following is a statement that Robert C. Fuller gave about Mesmer's grandiose method of operation:

> Mesmer would don a lilac-colored cape, play on his glass har-
> monica for the ostensible purpose of generating additional sanative
> vibrations, and prance about waving a wand at one patient after
> another. His patients graciously responded by falling into pronounced
> "crises" and emerged from this dramatic affair claiming cure.[11]

Benny does not wear a cape, but expensive designer suits. In the early days of his ministry he wore tuxedos, shirts with jabots, all matched with transparent high-heeled shoes containing dice or fishes! Benny does not play glass harmonica, but sings to excite people's emotions and make them ready to receive the anoint"Hinn"g. Benny does not wave a wand, but he waves his arm and blows on people. In both cases, their patients fall into "crises" and rise claiming cures.

In the days of Mesmer, medical men already understood the relationship between mood and cure. Mesmer had learned from his Viennese teachers about the healing properties of music.[12] Under his commands, musicians shifted from stormy to soft music. One of Mesmer's followers even testified to the exquisite sensitivity with which the mood of the patients changed as the mood of the music changed.[13]

Benny has learned his routine from Kathryn Kuhlman who also widely utilized mesmeric power. Very often during the course of a service Benny will order Sheryl Palmquist—the official organist of his ministry—to change the tempo of the music, and to quickly flow with him in the same spirit! I have myself remarked that people's reactions and moods change as the rhythm of the music increases or decreases. And he has some angelic music played whenever he prays, to give a feeling of divine atmosphere. He puts on—we have to admit—a very entertaining performance. His stage show rivals a Broadway production. Benny Hinn once confessed that he's an artist, that he's always been an artist.

Mesmer had an ability to throw subjects into a state between sleep and wakefulness. This condition was named the trance of mesmerism. This state grew in importance until it became the central point of his discovery. Mesmer became a master of it. Often his magnetism would cause the subject to undergo an even deeper state, a state referred to as *a crisis*.

Benny has the same ability, and gets the same results. He has become a master of the falling-down phenomenon which he calls "falling under God's power." It's camouflage for the same effect.

One remarkable note about Mesmer is that no matter how many hours he worked, he never seemed to tire.[14] Benny has often mentioned that when he operates under the "anointing" he does not tire.

Mesmer's disciples spoke of him in tones and in terms usually reserved for the deity.[15] The followers of Benny adulate him and his "anointing" in terms reserved to deity, whether in OCC or elsewhere.

Mesmer fully understood that his will dominated the will of the patient. He suggested to the patient that he would get well, convincing him of the fact, the cure coming about partly because he made the patient will the cure.[16] Having manipulated the patient's mind to obtain some results, and having gained the patient's confidence, Mesmer enticed him into becoming a follower. Some of his disciples even paid large sums of money to join his Society of Harmony.

Today Benny dominates his follower's will in a similar way. He repeatedly suggests to his crowds that they can all be healed, asking those who believe they are healed to come on stage and testify publicly. Then after gaining the confidence of the individual and of the crowd, he entices them into becoming partners to financially support his ministry. It's subtle but effective manner for recruiting financial supporters.

Are the Healings Genuine or Faked?

You may wonder if mesmeric treatments were always successful to cure patients. Mesmer, himself, achieved remarkable cures of functional disorders (where the function of some organ is affected, although there is no evidence of structural or organic changes). However, there were shortcomings.

> There was only one problem with mental treatment: It didn't always work. True, mesmeric treatments often gave instantaneous relief from ailments which had been deemed incurable. But in many cases the symptoms reappeared a few days later.[17]

Accounts of mesmeric cures in America are numerous. Thousands believed that such treatments were responsible for their recovery from back troubles, epilepsy, nervousness, liver ailments, stammering, insomnia, rheumatism, and blindness. Scores of followers reported prickly sensations or tingling, or some rush of energy going through them as the operator exercised the mesmeric ritual.

Today thousands attend miracle crusades and testify to feeling some tingling, numbness, or heat going through their body as a result of the "anointing" of a faith healer. In spite of repetitive warnings and evidence of fakery, too many people still persist in believing in those impostors.

The question we need to ask at this point is: Are those healings claimed by faith healers the results of genuine interventions of God, or the outcome of the power of mesmerism?

Cases concerning the mesmeric treatment of the blind, lame, and deaf are much less common. This is not surprising. Mesmer had realized that he could only treat those afflicted by mental or nervous disorders. His first concern was to determine whether the ailment was organic or functional. If the illness was organic, Mesmer would send the patient to a conventional doctor. If the illness was functional, he would prescribe a regimen of magnetism.[18] Ailments may also be classified as psychosomatic—ailments originating in or aggravated by the mind or emotions of an individual. James Wyckoff commented on Mesmer's honesty in these words:

> ...one reason for the high percentage of cure at his famous clinic was Mesmer's refusal to accept anyone whose ailment was organic rather than functional.... It was impossible to accuse him of duping his patients, for he openly announced that he could only help people suffering from nervous diseases, and he promised nothing.[19]

The faith healers, on the contrary, make no such distinction. They strongly suggest that anyone can be completely and permanently healed of any disease or sickness because the healers possess a divine "anointing" from God. But the cases they present as miraculous rarely stand up under scrutiny.

The methods used by faith healers differ slightly.

Benny Hinn, for instance, give several "words of knowledge" then invites those who have felt something to come up on stage. At this moment hundreds assemble in lines on each side of the platform. He has, however, appointed individuals who check people's claims in the audience. Their task is to determine if the "healing" passes their standard. You can be sure that if their outer physical appearance contradicts their healing claims, not much attention will be given to them. The person may be ignored and left standing in the audience. They will allow on stage only meticulously-screened cases which seem to "prove" that healings and miracles take place in their service.

Several theologians, ministers, and medical experts have tried to find some genuine evidence that people are completely healed and remain healed as a result of attending a faith healer miracle service, or by watching it on their television screen.

The truth is Benny, like other faith healers, cannot offer proof of genuine cases of healings or miracles as a result of their "anointing." Benny, or others, may say he does not heal, that the Holy Spirit does it through him; if it is the case, if anyone can be healed in his service, then why does he need to screen the healings?

The fact is that he and other faith healers capitalize on people's desperation and hide behind the name of God to build up their own empires—for which they would say or do anything to keep. They have a craving they need to satisfy. Here is what Vincent Buranelli relates about Mesmer's craving for recognition. Mesmer's treatment of a young woman, Franzl Oesterlin, who suffered from a form of psychosomatic illness, had brought him public attention.

> The Franzl cure gave him [Mesmer] a reputation as a healer. He took more patients, worked more cures, and became the talk of Vienna. While his fellow physicians became colder to him, those who flocked into his waiting room gave him what he craved—belief in...magnetism. That belief, since he was actually using the power of suggestion, naturally contributed to his continuing success. Partly it was a matter of faith healing, partly it was his skill as a hypnotist; but

Puységur's Tree

THE BETTMANN ARCHIVE

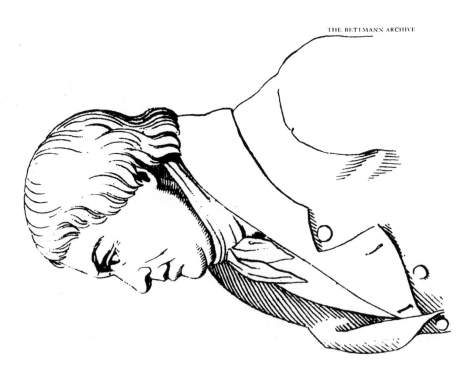

Franz Anton Mesmer

Miss Paradis's father entering Mesmer's apartment by force

Mesmer presiding over a magnetic séance

he told them it was…magnetism flowing through their bodies, and they accepted his explanation as absolute truth.[20]

Benny makes his follower believe that his "anointing" causes them to feel heat, numbness, tingling; and that his "anointing" makes them fall down individually or in groups. And people unquestionably believe his explanation. But his anointing is not of God, it is pure mesmerism. On top of that, Benny plays with his "patients" to make a show out of it like a ventriloquist plays with his puppet. He does not rank human dignity on a very high standard.

Mesmer needed his elegant settings because the aristocrats who came to the clinic would feel at ease in a type of room familiar to them; while the poor would feel that they were being lifted by Dr. Mesmer above the sordid life they lived. He knew the setting aided the cure.[21]

Dr. Hinn, an honorary title given by his good friend Oral Roberts, needs his elegant church and crusade setting. Because of the ambience, the paying partners who come to the crusade or church services feel comfortable and important to partake in his ministry. And the numerous poor and needy people who come full of hope and expectations, and the few that get the "chance" to be touched by the "great man" feel also that their spirit is lifted above the ordinary life they live.

Let me briefly comment on a man who was a contemporary of Mesmer. That man obtained the same results, perhaps with a different understanding. Surely, he did not use the same terminology. He held a position as a clergyman.

His name is Johann Gassner. A Swiss country man, seven years older than Mesmer, he received a Jesuit education and went on to become a Catholic priest. Gassner was widely acclaimed for his exceptional art of exorcism—a popular healing method at the time that enjoyed the theological and ecclesiastical backing of the Catholic Church.[22]

Gassner, as a young priest, experienced bouts of ill-health that seemed to intensify when he celebrated Mass, and so, he came to the conclusion that the devil attempted to deflect him from his calling. He, therefore, resorted to prayer and fasting in addition to a form of self-exorcism which brought relief from the aches and pain. Here is a very interesting account given by James Wyckoff:

> Calling on the Lord for help he was finally successful in ridding himself of his pain. In order to prove to himself that the devil had caused his illness, he commanded in the name of God that his pains should return. They did so and he was able to again exorcise them….[23]

It is also reported that he always spoke to his patients in Latin, and they responded to his directions, whether they knew the language or not.[24]

If this is not occult, how can we define it?

Is there a relation between Roman Catholicism, the faith healers, and mesmerism? I find it suspicious that people with similar backgrounds, driven by similar powers, but practicing under different labels, end up with similar results!

Investigation on Mesmerism

Two separate royal commissions investigated the practices of Mesmer and were astonished at the sight of patients going into all sorts of physical contortions. They reported that:

> These convulsions are marked by violent, involuntary movements of the limbs and the whole body, by constriction of the throat, by throbbing in the chest and nausea in the stomach, by rapid blinking and crossed eyes, by piercing cries, tears, hiccups and *uncontrollable laughter*. These are preceded or followed by a state of languor and daydreams, a type of abatement or even slumber...." [emphasis mine].[25]

You also might be aware of a new trend in the Christian world which is known as the laughing spirit. It's a mesmeric phenomenon mainly promoted by a man from South Africa named Rodney Howard-Browne. In the fall of 1992 he was invited to Benny's church. At the time, he had not yet gained too much popularity in the United States. We were quite bewildered by such unusual manifestations of laughter in the crowd; some were on the floor, others were still in the pews. Frankly, we were quite skeptical but mainly uncomfortable.

When Browne preaches, people start laughing uncontrollably, supposedly with the joy of the Lord. It becomes quite chaotic, for somebody next to you may roll on the floor, scream, and shout. These are other effects of mesmerism. Rodney Howard Browne orchestrates this practice in the same manner as Franz Anton Mesmer.

There is much about laughter in the Bible, but absolutely nothing like Browne's shows of manipulation. Influential religious leaders are quick to pinpoint the laughing spirit as another move of the Holy Spirit to support their theory of the supposedly revival of the last days.

When you see those faith healers behind the scenes you are really disappointed. We never expected perfection, but we were certainly not ready for such filthiness and corruption. The holy image they project on the television screen or on stage is only the mask that hides their true face.

Have you heard the famous and widely utilized Scriptures passage, "Do not touch my anointed ones" (Psalm 105:15)? This is a common reply from the fake faith healers and their followers when you raise a doubt about their integrity. It is an erroneous doctrine used to stay above any criticism. I am not touching God's anointed ones. I am exposing fake men and women who are deceptively using the name of God.

Madame du Barry, a comtesse and mistress of King Louis XV, has left this record in her *Memoires:*

> His [Mesmer's] lectures were attended by crowded audiences, and while some went away with the impression that a man who could unfold such wonders was a being superior to this world, many departed with the conviction that, if he were endowed with supernatural powers,

he derived them from Lucifer himself.[26]

This statement applies perfectly to today's fake faith healers.

CHAPTER FIVE
COME ON DOWN
YOU ARE THE NEXT...

Wednesday, July 1, 1992. We have been living in Orlando for a month, and all of us are very thrilled. And today, late in the afternoon, all the family gets ready to go to church for the 7:00 P.M. midweek service.

A few weeks earlier, I had had in my heart to start translating the bestseller book of Benny Hinn *Good Morning, Holy Spirit* from English to French. And as of that day, I had approximately five handwritten chapters. We owned no computer.

I had this urgent feeling that I needed to bring my manuscript to the church that Wednesday night.

Exactly why? I could not comprehend. But I felt undoubtedly persuaded that I had to bring my manuscript to the service.

We neared the church around 6:00 P.M. Stephan went to the children's ministry—he was a coordinator. My wife, our daughter, and I took our seats in the church. Yes, once again, all the seats in OCC were occupied. Approximately twenty-eight hundred people were present. Our new acquaintance Jeannine Welker came and sat next to us. This way, she said, she could practice her French.

The service commenced on time at seven o'clock. After the praise and worship, Benny began his habitual biweekly "news segment." During those minutes he related to the congregation some sifted information about the ministry. It is a common practice of his to relate stories about himself, or about the good old days. These are often a combination of a bad memory and a good imagination.

That Wednesday night he talked about his upcoming crusade in Toronto, Canada, on September 24-25. That crusade meant something special to him for he had started his ministry in that city many years earlier. Because of the importance of that crusade, Benny asked if any Canadians attended the service, and if so, would they please stand up. The three of us stood up, as did others.

First he asked other visitors what part of Canada they came from. Of course he got various answers. Then came our turn.

Benny asked us, "Where are you from?"

"We come from Montreal," I answered.

He then asked, "Are you visiting?"

Melanie, pushed by an emerging boldness, answered, "Pastor Benny, we are not visiting. The whole family has moved down here for the church."

His reaction was immediate, "Come on down on the platform, all of you." No need to say that the three of us rushed to the platform where we could shake hands with Benny Hinn himself.

"Why have you moved to Orlando?" he asked.

"God has led the four of us to move down here," I answered.

He further questioned, "Has the Lord revealed anything else to you?"

My wife promptly responded, "Yes, but we'll tell you in private."

I explained to him that the four of us were involved in Sunday school, and that Stephan was, at this very moment, volunteering at the children's ministry.

Benny turned towards the congregation and made this comment, "I am impressed. This family arrived here just a month ago, and they are already involved in one of the church ministries."

He then asked me, "Sir, what do you do for a living?"

"I'm a translator and interpreter, pastor," I answered.

"Well," he said, "why don't you translate my bestseller *Good Morning, Holy Spirit*, and when you are finished, why don't you also translate my book *The Anointing*."

Then I understood why I had brought my manuscript to the church.

I replied, "I have already started translating *Good Morning, Holy Spirit*, pastor. I even have the manuscript with me."

He could not suppress his surprise, "I want to see it."

Immediately Jeannine, who knew I had placed the manuscript in the seat compartment, brought it on the stage and gave it to Benny.

Benny asked Pastor Fred Spring, one of his associates for more than twenty years—a Canadian himself—and who had known us for a few weeks, "Fred, are you the one who talked to me about these precious people?"

Fred blushed all over, then shook his head sideways, answering, "No."

Then Benny asked the same question to Jeannine. She was the one who had talked to him about us.

Benny looked at the manuscript and seemed to be very pleased. As a young boy, he was taught by French-speaking nuns and monks in Jaffa; hence, his good knowledge of the French language.

He then asked the congregation to join him and they all prayed that we would quickly receive our immigration papers.

Benny added that he wanted to see the four of us in his private office that same night after the service. He then invited us to go back to our seats.

I will never forget the look on Fred's face that night, when Benny asked him if he was the one who had spoken to him about us.

This man, Fred Spring, had showed his real face. No man that possesses a pure heart gets, as Fred got that Wednesday night, such a blush over his face. He looked so red we thought he would explode.

The service continued and turned into one of those "Healing Services"; although it could be better characterized as a night in which Benny used his anoint"Hinn"g to manipulate people's emotions. In fact, he displayed his mesmeric practices.

When the service ended we walked to the front. After being checked and approved by Benny's bodyguards and assistants, they allowed us to go backstage and talk privately with him.

This in itself is quite an accomplishment, for you cannot talk to Benny Hinn after the services. As soon as he is finished preaching and makes the altar call, he is immediately surrounded by bodyguards who escort him to his backstage office. There he is unreachable, whether at the beginning or at the end of any service.

Benny seemed excited about the whole situation. He asked for our names and then said to my family, in front of his right-hand man Kent Mattox and few other staff members, "I'm going to help you get your working permits, and I'm going to put you to work. I had a long day, I'm tired, but I want you to call my personal secretary Nancy Pritchard first thing Monday morning. I want you to ask her to set up an appointment with me as soon as possible."

Benny demanded to know if I could interpret and speak French like the people from France do.

"Of course we can," my wife said with a beautiful Parisian accent.

He looked so happy about the whole thing. He seemed to enjoy the conversation.

The following morning I called Gene Polino—the church administrator—and asked him if we could use any of church computers, whether at day or at night. Mr. Polino refused my request, saying that all computers were utilized, even at night. But he never objected to the translations of Benny's books.

Therefore, we rented a computer to do the translation requested. We wanted to give him professional work. You cannot imagine how happy we felt. Benny had asked us before the whole congregation to translate two of his books; moreover he said in his office that he would help us get our working permits and that he would put us to work.

We should have known that when you are swept off your feet, it is time to go on your knees.

Unfortunately things did not turn out the way we were promised they would. The upcoming tribulations were going to reveal the real, the true face of Benny Hinn and his ministry.

Naturally the first thing I did Monday morning was to call Nancy—Benny's personal secretary. The first time I called, I got her voice mail. I do not know how you feel about it, but I find it very impersonal to converse with a machine. This appeared to be the procedure, however, so I left a very clear message.

She did not return my call. "Well," I said to the family, "Maybe she is very, very busy, too busy to call us back." So I called again, and again, and again. I must have left at least ten messages on her voice mail over a period of a few weeks. She never called back.

Let me tell you something. If secular companies were as rapid and as professional as Benny's ministry is in returning its phone calls, they would all go bankrupt. No customer would tolerate to be treated that way.

Nevertheless, I continued calling, and she continued not returning my calls. Days turned into weeks, and it was still impossible to get through.

Would you believe that one day the voice mail gave me this message, "Don't leave a message," simply because the voice mail had already reached its capacity—and it can hold 100 messages!

How is that for first-class service and courtesy towards the callers, Mr. Benny? I hope they had not received any emergency phone calls that day.

Since we could not obtained from his secretary the appointment requested by Benny himself, we decided to reach him by a different route. Here is how we attempted to do so.

We had been attending the daily 6:00 A.M. prayer meetings at OCC for a few weeks. Those meetings, supposed to be dedicated to prayer, were conducted by two different pastors: Fred Spring and Jim Edwards. Fred took charge on Mondays, Tuesdays, and Wednesdays; while Jim took over on Thursdays and Fridays.

Jim Edwards really dedicated his meetings to prayer. Pastor Jim is an honest man with a servant's heart, but his abilities are restrained by Fred's controlling spirit.

Sad to say, the meetings led by Fred were totally different. Fred had been an Assembly of God ordained minister for more than thirty years. He had been the senior pastor in a few churches in Canada and the United States. One of these churches numbered about three thousand members in Minnesota.

He had, as his executive director, helped Benny start his ministry in Canada, then later on came to Florida to work in Benny's ministry. But Fred, being a man who worked as a senior pastor almost all of his life, seemed to act in the same manner. The man still believed that at OCC, he headed a church.

During those one-hour prayer meetings, Fred would normally spend forty-five to fifty-five minutes talking about his souvenirs and experiences. We learned during those meetings that his daughter, some years before, had had mechanical problems with her car; so someone gave him a car. He also explained how he dealt with a lady whose phone calls disturbed him; once, while the lady talked on the phone, he put the phone aside, ate some cookies, then came back on the phone. The lady supposedly kept on talking without ever noticing Fred's absence!

The point I am making is that Fred exploited those meetings to talk about or do anything except what the meeting was called for, that is, praying. He is also a stubborn man. He had received some complaints about not leading a real prayer meeting but he did not like such comments. So once those critics had left the meetings, he would defend his position by raising doubts about their integrity.

I remember one incident involving Fred that really hurt our feelings. One morning after the prayer meeting, which Fred conducted in replacement of Jim Edwards, as we exited the church and started walk home, we encountered what is known as a Floridian rainfall. Believe me, it does not rain for a very long time in Florida; but when it rains, it pours.

So we were walking out of the church and into the rain, while our dear friend Fred was following us. He saw the rain, he noticed that we didn't have a car that day, nor an umbrella, but still he walked right by us.

Why should he bother to give us a ride home in his brand new Cadillac? After all, are we not members of the same church? This is the kind of first-class brotherhood that some members of Benny's pastoral staff show to the congregation.

One morning Fred opened his heart and declared his feelings to the group. "You know, Benny is still pretty young and sometimes he doesn't think before he opens his mouth. We should all pray and ask the Lord to give him more wisdom." He considered that at thirty-nine years old, Benny had less wisdom than him. This factitious remark, made during a Monday morning prayer meeting, referred to the previous day when Benny had called some of his first row members "dead ducks." Benny felt during the service that they were not showing enough interest in his anoint"Hinn"g. Perhaps, those "dead ducks" knew something that we ignored at the time.

Benny has a very dangerous tendency to say anything and everything that runs through his mind. It has before, and it will in the future get him into all sorts of problems.

Since we could not get our appointment via the regular channel—Nancy Pritchard—we decided to ask Pastor Fred. Since he had known Benny for more than twenty years, we felt he could talk directly to him about the problems we were facing in getting the appointment. Fred has his own little office in a trailer adjacent to the main church building. He refused an office in the building because he says, "I prefer not being close to the staff." He also gave us a very sound advice, "Don't trust anyone here." Well, it surely included him.

Fred's answer was something we could have never thought possible, "I would love to help you but I, myself, have to wait sometimes two or three weeks before I can talk to Benny."

We had also heard a rumor that we wanted to verify. So we asked him, "Is it true, Pastor Fred, that Gene Polino has forbidden you to talk to Benny; except for the time you and Benny are both on the platform?"

Fred's face blushed once again, he stammered, bowed his head and looked at the floor. He finally admitted it but replied, "Benny is too preoccupied with the crusades and what gravitates around. He doesn't want to be annoyed with the church or any kind of problem." In Benny's eyes, even his own church members and staff do not have much value.

This statement also proves a lot of things. The most important being that the real authority, the real boss in Benny Hinn's ministry is not Benny as he claims to be, but the church's administrator Gene Polino. Mr. Polino stands as a very, very powerful man, and whatever he decides, Benny agrees to.

So we did not get the help from Fred Spring we expected. We had to figure out how to obtain our appointment with Benny. And yet, we still hung on to the promises made to us. We still hoped that something would develop, that things would happen.

I continued calling the church. One day my phone call finally got through. I could talk to a real person—I got Nancy Pritchard on the phone. I was so surprised that for a few seconds I stood there speechless. At last I could explain the situation to her. I told her the complete story. But she told me to hold on, for she had Pastor Benny on another phone line; and she would ask him about our appointment.

I waited for what seemed hours, then she came back on the line and said, "Pastor agrees to meet with you. I only have to check his schedule and I will get back to you as soon as possible."

For once we had a decent and solid answer. Maybe this was the right time. We had been waiting for so long, maybe we would finally meet Benny Hinn.

Well, we were disappointed another time, for we never got any answer from Nancy. Either Benny lied when he said he wanted to meet us, or Nancy lied when she pretended he wanted to see us. It ended with the same result: we still had to wait.

I never thought that a man of his reputation could be that cruel, and at the same time, so immature. If Benny did not want to see us, he should have been mature enough to inform us of his decision.

I do not believe that we can find a container big enough to hold all the promises made, and all the meaningless words that people pronounce. If such a container existed, Benny and his staff would do more than their share of filling it to the top.

It is a blessing that we had a touch-tone telephone because if I had used a rotary phone, I would have mangled my fingers just by dialing the church phone number.

Since our arrival at OCC we had made new friends. Stephan and Melanie also became good friends with Kenny Smith. That friendship did not please Jeannine Welker for she wanted to control his leisure times. She believed that Kenny would marry her daughter Michelle. Jeannine saw our children as adversaries and opponents to her plans. You have to realize that with her daughter babysitting at Benny's home, and with Kenny Smith being Benny's personal bodyguard, Jeannine knew almost everything about Benny's home and ministry.

In some occasions, after he had driven Benny to the church, Kenny would come home and have breakfast or lunch with us. He also went jogging and worked out with Stephan.

Jeannine and Kenny—although they had close relationships with Benny—were not interested in pleading our cause to him. For they feared him or Gene Polino. It is a well-known fact that the latter forbids anyone of disturbing the "great man."

One morning Kenny came to our home. He was distressed, but mainly upset. He had just been fired as a personal bodyguard, not by Benny, but by the administrator, Gene Polino. Here is how Kenny related it.

Kenny had a long-time friend—a girl. Nothing was serious between them, they were just good friends. She had come up from Miami to pay him a visit. The administration of the church wanted to get rid of Kenny, so they tricked him by making up a story. They declared that he had slept with that girl. This is the reason Polino gave Kenny when he fired him. Even if he denied the whole story, the verdict was pronounced—no appeal was granted.

A short while earlier, Kenny had interrupted a private conversation between Gene Polino, Kent Mattox, and Nancy Pritchard. Mr. Polino was expressing his desire to close OCC in order to concentrate all their efforts on the crusades. After hearing this astonishing declaration in the corridor, Kenny tiptoed away from the scene hoping that no one had noticed his presence.

Fred had already mentioned Benny's attitude in favor of the crusades. Kenny's dismissal appeared to prove the existence of a plot involving Gene Polino.

Time seems to prove the veracity of that declaration. Benny Hinn's ministry holds on a monthly basis, since that time, more meetings than ever. This new way of management keeps Benny away and justifies, by his increased work load, more frequent absences from his flock in Orlando. The church then hired Gary Beesley as an associate pastor. He has the responsibility of preaching Sunday night and Wednesday night services. This way Benny preaches only on Sunday mornings.

The saddest part of Kenny's dismissal is that even if he worked as Benny's personal bodyguard, even if this man—Kenny Smith—would have given his life for the ministry; Benny refused to talk to him after he was fired. Kenny was not permitted to share his version of the story. Was Benny aware of the delicate content of Polino's private comment? Or was Benny hiding once again behind his administrator, thus approving his decision?

Kenny disappeared for a few days but returned shortly after wearing an OCC security guard uniform in the church. If he had really committed in their eyes an immoral sexual act, why did they give him a security guard position? If he cannot be trusted in one position, he cannot be trusted in another.

Shortly after, Benny Hinn had a new bodyguard named David. After a few weeks though, Kenny left the area. It is unconceivable that Benny refused to talk to a man who spent his entire days to serve, and to protect him at the cost of his life. And this guy—Benny Hinn—brags on the platform that he and his wife live like the Bible teaches us to do! He hides himself behind his personage.

When Benny told us on Wednesday, July 1, 1992, "Come on down," we did not know we would be the next ones to be seduced and betrayed by this man and by his administrator. One only needs to visit churches in Orlando and its suburbs to discover all the emotionally wounded people who used to attend OCC regularly. Churches are filled with people who have been deceived, seduced, and victimized by the "great man."

Once, Fred Spring commented about the church turnover and why people left in such great number. "This place here is a center, not a church. People come and go, hence the name Orlando Christian Center." He should have added, "And we do not really care."

You might want to ask all those who have been hurt at Orlando Christian Center how they feel about that comment. If OCC, as Fred says, is not a church, then why is it that they insist on people getting their membership and tithe number by holding monthly meetings specifically for this purpose?

Let me tell you about one of those victims. Everyone called her Auntie, a sweet lady in her mid-nineties. She attended OCC on a very regular basis. One of the first people in church, she would arrive around six o'clock on Sunday mornings. One day Auntie suffered from a very bad cold, and she could not refrain from coughing in the service. That cough, of course, disturbed and offended Benny Hinn, the "great man."

So Benny, without saying a word, but with a hateful look on his face, signaled one of his front row bodyguards to escort her out of the church. Poor Auntie, she was weeping. It was a sad moment. Auntie and her niece Eunice, like numerous other victims, left and went to another church in Orlando.

He should have prayed for the lady instead of forcing her out. After all, he brags about his healing ministry. I guess his anoint"Hinn"g could not overcome a simple cough!

Benny is a dangerous man for he becomes intolerant of those who do not accept his practices and doctrines without question. He makes his followers believe that he gets his orders directly from the Holy Spirit; thus, opposing Benny Hinn is like opposing God Himself. He does not believe in freedom of expression and, because he stands in a position of power, he condemns those who challenge him.

He surrounds himself in the church, even during the course of regular services, with six to eight bodyguards and backscratchers.

That sort of attitude by a pastor should not be tolerated by any member of a congregation. But who will dare to stand against Benny Hinn, especially in his church. The second you make an unusual sound, sycophants surround you.

These men sit in strategic places on the extremities of the first few pews. And when

Benny tells them to move, they better move. Otherwise they will be rebuked before the whole congregation, or worse, fired shortly after. And I thought slavery was illegal in the United States!

Those men maneuver under the supervision of David Delgado, a man who has been working with Benny for many years. This man serves Benny like a slave serves his master. Very often in church and before the whole congregation Benny said to Delgado, "David, it's very warm on the platform, go and fix that air conditioning and don't come back until it's really fixed. Hurry up and don't you dare do any diddle daddle." After his departure, Benny would say to the congregation, "Sometimes I'm not even sure if David's saved."

This is one of the very strong points of Benny's personality. He takes advantage of every situation to make sure that everyone in the church understands that he is "the boss." But some bodyguards, like Oscar, make you question their spiritual state, and that of the church.

But what unholy spirit really inhabits OCC?

What amazes me is that those who are really close to Benny, men like Kent Mattox and others, who are frequently touched by the "great man" in church show no "anointing" whatsoever. Neither does the "anointing" produce any fruit of the Spirit in them. However they become disagreeable just like Benny—for he transfers his bad spirits to them.

Let me tell you about Oscar. If you have watched the "Inside Edition" exposé, he is the chubby fellow who pushed away the journalist Steve Wilson. Mr. Wilson was desperately trying to approach Benny Hinn in the Philadelphia airport. It was a ugly scene, to say the least.

Oscar was working for Benny's ministry and then for some reason he disappeared. Some time later we saw him back in church, not as a bodyguard but as a simple spectator. During that Sunday evening service, Benny was in the business of casting out demons. So he made an altar call for those who needed deliverance from demons. Hundreds and hundreds of people answered the call. It scared me to know that so many demons were surrounding us! So Benny laid hands on people; some screamed, some cried, but they all fell down. A demonstration of mesmerism.

Then he called Oscar up on the platform and really levelled the guy. Benny told the crowd that ten demons had invaded Oscar during his sojourn out of the church. He had prayed for him just before the service; four demons had come out in Benny's office, the remaining six would come out now. Well, I did not know there were office demons and church demons! How can you sort them out? Benny added that their were about six people holding Oscar down while he prayed over him. Either the demons were very strong, or Benny and his clique were weak!

But what about our appointment?

The summer season had gone by, and I still desperately tried to get an answer from Benny's secretary. We could not understand that such a big ministry with so many staff members could give such lousy service.

The charisma, the strong personality of Benny Hinn, and the glamour that radiates from his television ministry and "Miracle Crusades" attract many people to OCC; but his real personality, his irresponsible attitude, his true face force many out of it. And a countless number of members, within six months, leave abused and deceived. Yes, this guy Benny Hinn, just like his peers, is really a fake.

In the next chapter I will show you the parallels and similarities between Benny Hinn's ministry and Jim Bakker's. You will realize that nothing is new under the sun; and that the same greedy spirit that guided Jim Bakker now guides Benny Hinn.

If they were true men of God, they would know that the love of money is a root of all kinds of evil, a source of all kinds of trouble. The Scripture tells us what a true man of God pursues in life, whether on stage or behind the scenes:

> "But you, O man of God, flee these things [covetousness, greediness] and pursue righteousness, godliness, faith, love, patience, gentleness" (1 Timothy 6:11).

And they say they are not in it for money!

CHAPTER SIX
THE ACADEMY AWARDS: THE JUDAS

A wicked man is the worst of creatures.

A wicked Christian is the worst of man.

A wicked minister is the worst of Christians.

For many, many years, numerous followers have dedicated a devoted affection and a blind submission to very well-known preachers who are supposed to be women and men of God. Those famous preachers have very wisely exploited their famous personality to lure and induce many well-intentioned and innocent people into their paths.

Today's contemporary faith healers act much like old-fashioned "medicine men" by dwelling on the fears and expectations of people. They are fakes and frauds practicing spiritual cure without a license. They propose antidotes that people believe are coming directly from God but are nothing more than mesmeric doses. The faith healers leave behind them a forlorn trail of emotional wreckages, illnesses, and diseases; it is sometimes worsened by negligence because of their lies.

During the period between 1800 and 1850, the intense religious fervor in America testified of the desire of popular demand to search for new ways of getting "the automatically operant Holy Spirit to descend and symbolize the start of the New Life."[1] It is not surprising that mesmerism entered into American cultural life. The mesmerists traveled from town to town on a circuit nearly identical to that of the revivalists, and similarly preached that problems plaguing humanity would continue as long as they refused to open themselves up to a higher spiritual power. Some came to hear about this new healing science out of sheer curiosity, but many came out of sheer desperation.[2]

This chapter proves that contemporary deceitful faith healers teach the same erroneous beliefs and use the same techniques as the real mesmerists of those days. Faith healers, who are also popular attractions, have learned how to wrap up very successful dramatic techniques that they afterwards use to minister to contemporary audiences.

Three members of the Faith Healers Hall of Fame have caught my attention. One is dead, Kathryn Kuhlman; the next one has been released from jail, Jim Bakker; and the third one is the fastest rising star, Benny Hinn. And the sad tradition continues.

These three obviously possess common links: a prestigious charisma; a show business personality; a very expensive standard of living; an urge to please a crowd; an unceasing desire to be admired and adulated; and a mastery of mesmerism.

Benny Hinn akin to Kathryn Kuhlman

It is a well-known fact that Benny Hinn admires Miss Kuhlman and her ministry. Indeed he has done so for years. The way he operates his ministry reflects the way Kathryn operated hers. To say that she greatly influenced Benny is an understatement. Let me point out some of the evidence.

Everyone in Miss Kuhlman's office acted like an automatic machine. Here is what Jamie Buckingham writes in his book *Daughter of Destiny.*

> I talked with a number of people who had visited the foundation offices and many said the same thing: "Robots! They are all robots in there…. They don't think. They just follow the behavior pattern which she has programmed into them."[3]

I myself walked quite often through the offices of Benny's ministry, and let me tell you that its employees also resemble robots. They worry especially about losing their job and picture any newcomer as a threat to their position. They work as robots, hoping that the "great man" will note some kind of special gift in them, or maybe that he will greet them.

Miss Kuhlman had a mystical authority over people. Even those in charge were not in charge when Kathryn was around.[4]

Every time I have seen Benny ministering in a service outside of his church, even if he is only a guest speaker, Benny has to be in charge. For instance, it happens every time he is invited on the Trinity Broadcasting Network. Things must go his way, and Paul and Jan Crouch would certainly not oppose him. He is a sure investment.

Jamie Buckingham talks in his book about Kathryn's personal devotional life. Here is what he says:

> Kathryn often made public claims that she read no books but the Bible…. However, her desk was filled with underlined copies of books by Andrew Murray and Jessie Penn Lewis…. Of even greater interest were the printed sermons by Norman Vincent Peale I discovered in the bottom drawer of her desk. Peale and Kuhlman seemed poles apart, yet she obviously admired the famous pastor and at one time or another in her life probably probably drew from his excellent storytelling ability.[5]

This statement worries me a lot. We all know that Peale is considered the father of the positive thinking teaching, an erroneous theology because it affirms that if you think in a positive way, you can get anything you want, your way. Did you know that Norman Vincent Peale held a thirty-three degree Freemason position? Peale exploited a Christian front to propagate his mystical messages, and people believed it.

Miss Kuhlman admired Peale; Benny admires Miss Kuhlman. A person that you admire will inevitably influence you one way or another. The message they deliver, however, may not be divinely inspired as it is claimed.

Kathryn loved fine, expensive things, and it was not unusual for her to go into an exclusive clothing shop and spend $3,000 at one time. Her lifestyle demanded an extensive wardrobe.[6]

Benny proceeds the same way when he puts his power shopping abilities into action. He lives the lifestyle of the rich and famous, not the lifestyle of the meek and Jesus.

> "I am the only one who knows the direction of the Holy Spirit in those miracle services. If these men want to see miracles, they'll just have to fall in line, or get out. It's just like that!" boasted Kathryn Kuhlman.[7]

Benny believes he is unique, that no one can match the "anointing" he pretends he has received from above. He cherishes his favorite citation, "You want the anointing? But you don't now the price I had to pay. You have to die to yourself." Then he goes on with his good storytelling ability declaring things such as, "I must do this now. The Holy Spirit would not allow me to continue." It is as if he has a direct phone line, like he is an elite to whom God talks.

In her healing services Miss Kuhlman insisted on the presence of luminaries behind her onstage.[8] She had also a special love for doctors and wanted them either onstage or in the front rows of the auditorium.[9] The same was true with priests and nuns, especially if they were in habits.

> "Nothing thrilled Kathryn more than to have thirty or forty Catholic clergymen, especially if they wore clerical collars.... Somehow it seemed to lend authenticity to what she was doing..."[10]

Anyone who has seen on television or attended a Benny's "Miracle Crusade" has noticed the presence of dignitaries on or close to the platform. And he always brings with him on the crusades two to four doctors that he sits onstage or in the first rows. For the followers, the presence of spiritual fat cats vouches for Benny's credibility, and the presence of medical doctors authenticates his healing credentials. Bear in mind that these doctors have been hand-picked by the "great man" himself.

Benny proudly shows in his "Miracle Crusades", held in Catholic strongholds, that he is surrounded by Catholic priests and nuns. I do not believe that the presence of nuns and priests in collars or any other religious representatives bring any authenticity or any legitimacy to a healing. He invites priests and other religious leaders only to draw their followers to his crusades, and thus increase the attendance.

Kathryn also enjoyed talking about the movie stars—both the sleazy and strong—who attended her miracle services.[11]

I have heard Benny talk many times about the presence of Dyan Cannon and her friends at his crusades. He even waited for an invitation to go to Miss Cannon's house for dinner. She was supposed to invite some Hollywood celebrities such as Barbra Streisand, Arnold Schwarzenegger, and others. Indeed, Benny seeks recognition.

Great importance is given to the musical aspect, the songs heard in the healing crusades like "Hallelujah" and "He touched me"; the bus system to bring people to the crusades; even the singer Jimmy McDonald that Benny employs now; all these factors are identical to the ones Miss Kuhlman employed. Benny even pronounces "Jeeeesus" the same way she did.

Benny Hinn also faces the same problems Kathryn had to deal with. In spite of the popular belief among his followers, Benny struggles to medically authenticate that miracles really take place in his ministry.

Despite their constant assurances, no credible evidence of medically authenticated or genuine healings can be found. The healing cases that faith healers cite as evidence are not bona fide cases. Unfortunately, there still exists a persistent belief among their flock that miracles and healings regularly take place.

Where are the obvious organic diseases being healed in their "Miracle" services, like victims of accident who've become quadriplegic or who've lost limbs? What is presented and publicized by faith healers are mostly functional ailments, psychosomatic disorders, or cases of organic diseases which have been through surgery or other medical treatments. Organic diseases involve alteration in the structure of an organ, whereas functional ailments are caused by the malfunction of an organ under the control of the nervous system. If the malfunction is corrected, the symptom or disease can be relieved.

Where can we find the validation of those healing ministries? After all, years and years of ministry should produce irrefutable proof of the manifestation of God's work in their midst. In this case, broken limbs restored, missing limbs that grew back, muscular dystrophy reversed, all instantly and completely before the camera, should be found.

In an attempt to provide proofs of healing in his ministry, Benny Hinn submitted on September 4, 1992, to the Christian Research Institute (CRI), three healing testimonies bearing doctor's records and documentation. The three cases were examined by CRI's medical consultant Preston Simpson, M.D.[12] Benny also divulged in those days his ambition to publish in 1993 a book containing authenticated healings resulting from his "anointed" ministry. And he did.

Here is the brief description of those three cases that one can find in *Christianity in Crisis:*

Case 1: Colon cancer. A careful examination of the medical records supplied by Hinn reveals that the malignant tumor had been surgically removed...rather than miraculously healed.

Case 2: Lupus and related disorders. This is a particularly interesting case in that lupus is well-known to go into remission spontaneously for years at a time. This naturally makes miraculous healing difficult to verify. What can be verified are the *effects* of lupus—in this case damage to the sacroiliac joint—which was definitely not healed.

Case 3: Spinal tumor and various cancers. This case really has problems...the records reveal that the spinal tumor began shrinking some three months *prior* to Hinn's Miracle Invasion Rally...the tumor was still present—not healed—months after the alleged "healing."[13]

If these are the strongest cases Benny Hinn could supply—and presumably they were—he should have brought to an end his allegations of God's manifestations in his ministry. The results of all this are simple: He has nothing concrete that proves beyond any reasonable doubt that God is in the midst of his healing ministry. His anoint"Hinn"g is disguised mesmerism, pure and simple.

Following his ambition he came out in 1993 with Lord, I Need a Miracle. And he entrusted Dr. Donald Colbert—a regular on his "Miracle Crusade"—with the foreword of the book. In it Doctor Colbert describes two cases as "extremely impressive" and "carefully documented."[14] Strangely enough, these two are the same weak healing "proofs" as cases one and two submitted previously to CRI in September 1992.

I will give you a case of mental treatment that Franz Anton Mesmer used in an attempt of proving his theories to his compatriots. Even after an apparently successful treatment that should have strengthened his credibility, Mesmer still lacked the recognition of his theories among his fellow doctors in Vienna. The opportunity of proving his case shortly presented itself.

Mesmer offered his help to heal the blindness of a teenage girl named Maria Theresa von Paradis. Her story was that she had lost her sight due to a shock at the age of four years old. Mesmer decided to help because her condition seemed to be the result of some nervous disorder. He had said that he could not cure organic blindness; if the optic nerve was damaged, he would be powerless.

Despite her handicap, Maria was the idol of musical Vienna because she phenomenally mastered the piano. Maria so impressed Mozart that he later composed a concerto in her honor.

Mesmer's continuous treatments gradually improved her condition; Mesmer had restored much of her sight and healed her nervous condition in general. The improvement should have brought wide celebration; instead, it produced anguish because Miss Paradis no longer played as beautifully—for she now watched her fingers on the keyboard. Her diminished talent now troubled her parents and herself. James Wyckoff comments:

> It was becoming evident that Maria Theresa had felt calmer and more peaceful before her sight was restored. Her world had been a blind world, but safe. All her ideas and values had now to be readjusted. The girl was clearly not happy with the world she was beginning to see.[15]

The whole situation caused quite a stir. A commission, formed of medical men, was eventually appointed to investigate Mesmer's alleged cures. One even admitted on two occasions that Maria was able to see. But the commission finally rejected her cure and Mesmer's work.

The doctors turned Maria's father into a furious man which led him to demand the release of his daughter from Mesmer's clinic. The whole chaos and confusion were enough to ruin his daughter's confidence and emotional stability. It was all over. Maria was blind again. The case led to Mesmer's expulsion from the faculty of medicine and his departure from Vienna. In early 1778 he left for Paris.

This case is similar in many ways to many false healings that Benny and other faith healers present as a result of their "anointing." Generally in healing services honest people, experiencing high emotional feelings created by the environment and doses of mesmerism, will declare that they are healed from their sickness. As with Mesmer's treatments, people may enjoy improvement of their condition, but the moment they come down from their exalted experience, the slightest emotional shock they receive will bring them back to their initial condition, perhaps worse.

Those who trust their lies do not realize they are seduced by glamorous displays of excitement. Those charlatans, by deliberately misrepresenting facts to innocent people, prove that their goal is more valuable than anything else.

Benny Hinn akin to Aimee Semple McPherson

Benny even admitted he frequented the grave sites of both Kathryn Kuhlman and Aimee Semple McPherson to get the "anointing" from their bones.[16] In *Charisma* magazine, he also admits that he visited Miss Kuhlman's grave site. Benny says, "I cannot deny that, while I was there praying, the presence of God was so strong that I almost fell under the power."[17]

Since I mentioned Aimee Semple McPherson, let me tell you about her. Aimee was a very well-known preacher in the 1920's and 1930's. She was known to have lived a very disorderly life. Her first husband passed away; she married again, her second husband divorced her; she remarried a third time, but her third husband divorced her.

She once disappeared for more than a month. When they found her, she claimed she had been kidnapped. After an investigation by the legal authorities, evidence showed Aimee had actually enjoyed a love holiday with a former employee in Carmel, California. The State even took her to court on that matter, but they rested their case. Nevertheless, Aimee most certainly succeeded in receiving the publicity she desired.

Aimee was also deeply involved with showbiz personalities and Hollywood movie stars who frequented her church. One of those stars, Anthony Quinn, whom at one period interpreted her into Spanish, said that one day he could not contain his fear, "...she put her hand on my shoulder and an electrical charge went through me." In his biography, *One Man Tango*, Quinn relates some interesting facts about his first visit to Mrs. McPherson's church:

> "Finally, a distant figure with bright red hair and a diaphanous gown crossed to center stage. We were well back in the crowd, but I could sense a *mesmerizing presence*." [emphasis mine][18]

As he later became more involved with her, Aimee told him that he would be a great preacher, lead his own congregation, and accomplish immense things.[19] A strong statement issued by a well-known minister that is yet to be fulfilled. Having reached the honorable age of eighty years old, the odds are against "Pastor" Quinn ever seeing this prophecy come to pass.

Mrs. McPherson's church, named Angelus Temple, and built in the late 1920's—an era of a very deep and penurious financial crisis—cost millions of dollars. She has left as an heritage a denomination called Church of the Foursquare Gospel. But one of the most astonishing facts about Aimee Semple McPherson is the way she was buried. Mrs. McPherson was laid to rest in an ornate casket equipped with a live telephone![20]

Benny has such an admiration for those individuals that he even visited their graves. Perhaps, the reason why he visited their grave site was to acquire their spirits to make more money!

One question remains unanswered: Did Benny bring with him his portable cellular phone?

Benny Hinn akin to Jim Bakker

Now that I have established resemblances and similarities between Mesmer, Kuhlman, McPherson and Benny; let me concentrate on the many parallels and analogies between Jim Bakker's ex-ministry and Benny Hinn's continuing ministry, not forgetting their mesmeric resemblance.

For the public in general, Jim Bakker is not considered a faith healer. In the public eye, Jim is a fraud for having fooled around with tens of millions of dollars. Nevertheless, it is reported that for the faithful who went to Heritage USA or attended healing services when he preached elsewhere, the full power of his calling was evident.[21] Jim, however, refrained from televising the most eccentric effects, because he feared losing some of his viewers. He also attended Kathryn Kuhlman's miracle service in Pittsburgh, and even interviewed her on *The 700 Club*.

Doug Oldham, Jim's best friend, chief gospel singer and cohost of the PTL show, said about Jim, "The guy mesmerizes you." In his autobiography, *Move That Mountain!*, Jim describes the moment he stretched out his hand to pray over a woman with cancer, "…it appeared a bolt of lightning shot from the tips of my fingers and hit her. Her body was literally picked up and hurled through the air."[22] Patients of mesmerists have professed to seeing emanations of magnetism streaming from the operator's hands. Jim Bakker has been inhabited by and has also exploited the mesmeric power.

Hundreds of thousands of people sincerely believed that they were doing God's work in sending money to Jim's ministry.[23]

Hundreds of thousands of people believe in Benny's ministry today. Many—but not enough—of them change their mind after attending his church, where they see more of his real nature.

Jim and Tammy Bakker did not keep very good relations with their immediate family. Although they lived in the same area, Jim's parents never visited Jim and Tammy's house over a period of almost a year, nor did Jim and Tammy visit Jim's parents.[24] Jim did not seem to care too much for his folks.

Benny shares with his kinfolks a relation I may call different. Willie Hinn is responsible for the mother's well-being because that is the way Mr. Constandi Hinn—the patriarch—wanted things to be done after his death. I always wondered why this honor was not granted to Benny, the oldest son of the family.

During the two years we spent at OCC, we saw the mother of Benny only twice in church; when the special guest James Robison preached, and on another special occasion. Benny never spoke about his brother Willie, who also pastors a church in Orlando. Christopher Hinn—also a brother—attends the services at OCC on very rare occasions. And if he does, he always comes in at the last minute. Sammy is a member of Benny's pastoral staff, and was the only regular until he became an evangelist. Michael, the youngest son of the Hinn family, does not attend nor visit the church of his brother Benny. We did not see Michael in OCC even once in two years. Benny has also two sisters, living in Toronto, Canada, but we never saw them either.

Henry Hinn, who pastors a church in Vancouver, Canada, makes it a point of honor to talk about brother Benny almost every time he preaches. He even pushes it to a point close to idolatry. On the other hand, Henry never misses an occasion in his sermons to make fun of and ridicule his brother Benny. There is something very contradictory in Henry's behavior.

Jim and Tammy Bakker practiced the art of "power shopping."[25] Power shopping is the most expensive way to shop because you do not buy in singles, you buy at least half a dozen of each item that you like, be it shoes, suits, ties, dresses, or accessories. You just do not look at the price tags. One of Jim's favorite haberdasheries was Dallas' Galleria store called Beylerian. In 1985 he bought $3,000 worth of suits and accessories. When indecisive about the color of shirt he wanted, he solved the problem by buying six shirts, each a different color. He has been known to purchase ten to twenty suits in one outing.[26]

Well, Benny perfected that art, and even patronizes the same store—Beylerian. Kenny Smith who used to travel with Benny everywhere told me that the "great man" bought, while in Dallas, twelve ties retailed $200 each, and in one single outing. And Benny buys his suits and his shoes in the same price extravaganza.

The prophet Amos denounced luxury and urged the people to care for the poor of the land. He particularly condemned their expensive houses (Amos 3:15; 5:11), their complacency (6:1), and their costly parties (6:3-6; 8-10). The rich got their money by exploiting the poor (5:11-15); yet, those wealthy people were religious and faithfully participated in the temple services (4:4-5; 5:21-27). Their religiosity was only a masquerade to cover their sins.[27]

I know one employee of OCC who endured serious financial difficulties because her working hours had been drastically reduced. She worked as a school teacher, and also volunteered as church usher. The church administration reduced her weekly working hours so that they would not have to give her full-time status and its related benefits. She was already struggling with low-wage pay checks, but with that reduction she just could not pay her bills anymore. Fewer $200 ties in your closet and you could have helped her, Mr. Benny!

Both Jim and Tammy could be brutal to the people serving under them.[28]

Many, many times I have witnessed the verbal brutality Benny exercises against people in his own church.

To Jim, people seemed to be dirt and dispensable, except the few people who were close to him.[29]

Benny treats people like dirt, like garbage. One incident occurred in Benny's church during a regular Sunday night service. It developed while he operated under the "anointing," or was it the anoint"Hinn"g? Let me detail the incident to you.

When you walk into Orlando Christian Center, you observe that a section located in the far right corner of the sanctuary is reserved for folks in wheelchairs. During the services, the house is always standing room only.

So during the course of that particular service, while Benny operated under the "anointing," one of the ushers—a sweet old man who looked like Colonel Sanders—had to wheel one of those persons to the restrooms. Of course he wheeled her back to her place using, obviously, the same aisle of the church. At that moment Benny, seeing that someone dared to move while he preached, yelled at the usher and treated him like an old piece of rag. I'm sure the poor man wished he could have hid himself between the carpet and the cement floor.

What a lovely way to treat a human being, a brother who gives hundreds of benevolent hours to the church. And this kind of behavior from the "great man" happened quite often while we attended OCC.

In those instances he liked to say to the offender, "Don't grieve the Holy Spirit." Does Benny really think that a person walking in the church grieves the Holy Spirit so awfully, but that his own yelling doesn't?

Jim did not care about the workers. Here today, gone tomorrow was fine with him.[30]

For nine years Benny had in his video department a lady who had started as a camera operator, and worked her way up. One day he asked her how she really perceived the ministry. The lady told him very honestly what she felt in her heart. Guess what? He fired her right there on the spot, and her husband who also worked in church got the same treatment the following day. I wonder what happened to them afterwards.

Michael Richardson, a former bodyguard of Jim Bakker, mentions that the people who worked at PTL were almost all very sincere, dedicated people. Michael describes Jimmy Swain, general manager of Heritage USA, as a really good man dedicated to the ministry, but overworked to exhaustion. He did not ask for extravagant gifts or high-style living. He was good to the partners and the people there. He had a heart open to people.[31]

The working staff in Benny Hinn's ministry are (well, almost all of them) very sincere and very dedicated employees. Pastor David Palmquist is really a sincere man, with a genuine pastor's heart. He loves people and people love him. David stands among the pastors as one who will dare to walk in the church before a service and take time to hug, shake hands, and chat with ordinary people. David has truly a servant's heart. This man took time to listen to our problems, and he even cried with us over our troubles and miseries.

Numerous workers left their lucrative jobs to come and get involved at PTL, because they felt Jim was chosen by God for some special mission, and they wanted to be part of it. They seemed not to pay attention to his extravagant lifestyle.[32]

The situation in Benny's ministry is an exact replica of Jim's. A lot of people have made big financial sacrifices to move to Orlando in order to attend OCC.

Some of the newcomers have found work in the ministry. Many are paid low wages but they hang in there just to sit under the anoint"Hinn"g and listen to the flamboyant teachings. Strangely enough, they do not seem to care if Benny drives expensive vehicles, or if he wears expensive designer suits.

Michael says this about Jim Bakker at PTL:

> Jim would say, 'Christians deserve the best of everything.' His message was, Hey, you can have everything you want. And money is nothing. God is everything, but money is nothing. So send me all your money and let me spend it. God will take care of you. That was kind of the philosophy he preached.[33]

Benny works it out in a different way but the goal is the same—to obtain people's money. He declares that everything we do for God should be done first class. He also says that Christians are the children of God and for that reason they deserve the best. Benny will not ask for money as bluntly as Bakker did. He has learned to be more subtle. Every single service he preaches for at least fifteen minutes that if you faithfully honor God with your tithes and offerings, God will prosper you. If not, well…he affirms you won't be blessed. Then he tells the ushers to pass the offering bags, while the crowd is musically entertained.

Strangely enough, I know people who have faithfully given their tithes to Benny's church but have been struggling financially ever since. We ourselves gave them money with a pure heart but we never received, while we were there, the harvest that Benny loved preaching. We gave because we were fooled by his false teaching—give in order to receive later, not give to bless others.

One fact about Jim Bakker is simply scandalous. And something similar happened to us and others in Benny's ministry. You might have never heard this story, or may have never thought it could happen in those "beautiful" Christian ministries. Jim's former bodyguard writes:

> Jim got on the television pleading for people to come work on the hotel. He had to have good carpenters, he said, and he didn't care where they came from. There was food, shelter, good jobs, he said, good-paying jobs…. I remember one couple that I talked to. They had come from Texas. The man and his wife hadn't had that much to start with, but they had heard the television plea…. When they get to PTL, there are no openings. So he is stuck without any money. So what does he do? He doesn't have the money to get back home. He doesn't have *anything*.
>
> He wanted to talk to Jim, but Jim wouldn't see him. I talked to him for about an hour. This guy was standing there crying like a little baby and telling me what he and his wife had been through.[34]

And as you have realized so far, we suffered a similar situation. When Benny asked us on stage to translate his books—which he did not pay for—and when we talked to him after that memorable service on July 1, 1992, Benny said he would take care of our working permits and put us to work. We did not ask him for any favor, or any privileges. Benny is the one who committed himself, the one who made the promises.

I witnessed an incident in the OCC lobby that relates to this. A poorly dressed man, a carpenter, came to the church receptionist and asked to talk to the administrator. He had done, few months earlier, some work for the ministry and had still not been paid. The man was in tears. He had no money, and that sum owed by OCC was overdue. The man had to beg to be paid. I am convinced that the ministry pays its broadcasting invoices faster than they paid this fellow.

Benny also finds a great satisfaction in ridiculing people's situations. On in many occasions during the Sunday services, he had those with financial problems stand up in the church because he said, "God has shown me to pray for those who have financial problems, stand up and we'll pray to break that spirit of poverty." I even remember that on some occasions he asked a few of those standing what their needs were. But he always passed us by.

I am amazed that God would show Benny to pray for the indigents, without showing him to fulfill the promises he had made to us. As far as I know, none of those who stood up in these occasions has seen their financial situations greatly improved after the "great man" prayed for their needs.

Franco, for instance, is a very close friend of Benny, and one of his bootlickers who jumps on the stage at the end of every service to "protect" Benny against the Christian brothers and sisters who would like to talk to him! Franco had been faithfully paying his tithe in that church. The last time we saw him in Orlando in May 1994, he had lost his business and was on the brink of losing his house. Why did Benny not help him?

Let me tell you a little more about Jim Bakker's true face. One day he decided to buy a Rolls-Royce. He and Tammy Faye had owned one before, but they had given it up because of the pressure of disapproval. So he bought himself a Rolls for $57,000, and the next day he bought Tammy Faye a 450 SL Mercedes-Benz for $50,000.[35] Here is the "unknown story" about Jim and Tammy's car purchases:

> On television Jim said that he felt like he deserved the personal Rolls, that he had worked so hard and that he and Tammy Faye had bought it with their own money.
>
> Not more than three months earlier, I heard him tell a staff meeting that the ministry was in such bad financial shape that he and Tammy had put all their savings back into it. Yet they had the money to go out and spend $100,000 on cars![36]

Benny owned a Mercedez-Benz 500 SEL—a car which costs over $100,000. Following the national exposé on *Inside Edition* (more details in Chapter 11) in March 1992, he sold it to make a good impression on the public. A car dealer supposedly gave him a brand new Lincoln luxury car to replace it.

The majority of you, however, ignore that shortly after, Benny was driving a brand new white Range Rover vehicle. Price list: approximately $55,000. We saw him driving it out of the church's parking lot, shouting in our direction, "God bless you." But he would not have dared to stop and talk to us.

So he replaced the Benz for an American car to calm his American fans, but got himself a Range Rover—a British vehicle! Too great a temptation, Mr. Benny? And that is not including the family van his wife drives to go to the health food store, or to bring the children to the church academy.

Benny has often boasted in church that he labors very hard, and that the only money he withdraws from the church is his salary. Let me clear up the matter here. If his books reach the bestsellers list, is it not because he uses the platform of the church built with people's money? And he exploits the air time of the TV ministry paid by the partners to promote book sales.

He also says that all the luxury items he buys are paid with the royalties of his books. But his ex-bodyguard Kenny Smith confided to us that his power shopping expenses are put on the church credit account.

Jim and Tammy were living the television screen one way and their private lives another.[37]

Benny shows on secular and Christian television an image that stands in total contrast to his private life. I have already showed you some insights of his ministry, but more will follow. Jim had tried to make people feel that they were not as good as he was, that they were low in the eyes of God, and that he was God's chosen one.[38]

And Benny succeeds in making people believe that they are not anointed, as he is. He keeps telling them, "You don't know the price I had to pay, you must die to yourself." Strangely enough, Kathryn Kuhlman and Aimee Semple McPherson utilized the same type of statement. Benny Hinn, like other faith healers, does not even understand the real meaning of his favorite citation, "You must die to yourself."

When *Channel 6 NEWS* interviewed Benny in March 1992, the reporter Tony Pipitone asked him, "Do you fear that you're gonna go the way of the Jimmy Bakker and the Jimmy Swaggart?"

Benny answered, "No. And the reason for it is because we are very careful with the way we are financially, morally. Our books are clean."[39]

Notice that he did not talk about the most important aspect of any Christian organization: the spiritual state of his ministry. Benny, in the same manner as Kathryn, determined a long time ago that the best way to face an unpleasant situation is to simply pretend it does not exist.

The treasure of Heritage USA was the mailing list housed along with the computers, the mail operation, and the executive offices in a building called World Outreach Center.[40]

Besides his "Miracle Crusades" in the United States, Benny has increased the frequency of his crusades overseas including some special projects to his work load. Therefore he has added a new name to his ministry. OCC is now known as the World Outreach Center!

Jim Bakker liked fruits, especially bananas.[41]

Benny Hinn mentioned on stage that he was eating an average of ten bananas a day! And that this regimen kept him going and slim. He took from Jim Bakker even the little things.

After revealing all those parallels between Jim Bakker and Benny Hinn, it would not be fair if I did not write about the sole difference between them.

Jim always had, except for a short period of time in his ministry, his wife Tammy Faye by his side. If you saw Jim, automatically you would see Tammy. She was one of the reasons their ministry skyrocketed as few others did. She holds also a major share of responsibility in the crash of PTL.

Benny, on the contrary, does not comprehend the necessity of having his wife Suzanne, whom he calls "bulldog" because of her English roots, constantly at his side. In return, she calls him "terrorist" because he hails from the Middle East. He does not want her in the facade of the ministry, except very rarely, despite the fact that she is an ordained minister. He wants the whole attention; he does not want to share his fame.

He declared on stage in OCC that when Suzanne and the children accompany him in a crusade, they do not lodge in his first-class hotel. He explains his awkward decision by saying that he needs to be alone in his hotel room to pray. He does not want to be disturbed. However he accepts his close friends, Gene Polino, Kent Mattox, Jim Cernero, Charlie, and a few others in the same hotel.

Perhaps this explains why Suzanne prefers to stay home and take care of the children. But where is the urge? She has more babysitters and servants than she has children.

Now let me explain why I have entitled this chapter The Academy Awards: The Judas.

In Hollywood, when the time arrives to give the Oscars, the committee gets together and votes for the various nominees. The golden awards are assigned to the very best of the best in their own specific category.

Well, in this case, the jury has unanimously come to one conclusion. To all the nominees: Benny Hinn, Kathryn Kuhlman, Jim Bakker, and Aimee Semple McPherson, I award a trophy. To each and everyone of those fake faith healers, I give The Judas.

This award truly reflects the name it bears. The jury awards it to those considered, by a lot of honest people, to be to Christ and all of his followers, traitors and betrayers like Judas the Lost.

Judas, even though he was one of the Twelve, never believed in Jesus (John 6:66-71). He would not have been chosen, but for the Scriptures to be fulfilled Judas was numbered among the Twelve (13:18), but not kept (17:12).[42] These Judases, display a frightening example of how one can use the name of God to earn a living.

CHAPTER SEVEN
IT'S A SIN TO TELL A LIE

We track down great resemblances between the fake faith healers and the contemporary fake prophets. The similitudes rely not only on the fact that, even if they use the name of God in vain and pretend serving Him, their fruits are poisonous; but they also lean on the fact that they operate in the business of counterfeit, and that their operations are nothing more than mesmerism.

Since the 1980s, a new dimension has been added to the religious world: the prophetic movement. In Orlando we came in contact with such a group. Some of the leading figures of this movement in the State of Florida are Randi and Cathy Lechner. Many others practice their prophetic gift under mesmeric power, not only in the United States but also worldwide.

Randi has been promoted as a prophet under the ministry of Bill Hamon. Cathy began her prophetic ministry in a meeting when her husband told her, "It is your turn Cathy, I want you to prophesy on that lady."

Bill Hamon and his disciples believe that all personal prophecies are conditional; that is, prophecies can be decreased, adulterated, or even canceled. What they really say is, "The prophecies we give you may or may not come to pass, and that may depend on you or some other circumstances."

The Bible however declares that you will judge the honesty of a prophet when his prophecies come to pass, regardless of the person or circumstances. If it does not come to pass, the Lord has not spoken; the prophet has spoken presumptuously.[1] Bill Hamon and his disciples simply try to avoid the ultimate test of honesty found in the same book they pretend to honor and teach.

The Lechners performed in the Orlando area at the Winter Park Civic Center. They held their meetings three times a month, on Tuesdays and Thursdays. But in those meetings they never ministered together.

Cathy's meetings always attracted a big crowd. The place they rented was always filled to capacity; mainly by her feminine clientele, or you may say her "fan club." Despite her smiling personality she occasionally had a strange look on her face when she walked in the room. She would stare at people with eyes that I cannot really describe. It was as if she would scrutinize the people's behavior and mesmerize their emotions.

Her faithful followers, present at each of her meetings, had great expectations. Among her faithful fans was Freida Bower, the co-founder of the local Christian television station WACX-TV, and a good financial provider for the ministry. And at each service Cathy never missed the chance to acknowledge Freida's presence. I presume that the other visitors were not worthy of recognition. The majority of the followers were

OCC members. We regularly saw Sue, the wife of Charlie McCuen—Benny's crusade coordinator and regular stage catcher—and Jacqueline, a long-time babysitter at Benny's home.

The devoted admirers longed for the favored instant, that is, the final part of the meeting where they would receive a prophecy from Cathy. Some are bound to receive their regular potion of divination, and to unwillingly live and conduct their lives according to the prophecies they receive.

Randi, in contrast to his wife, attracted smaller crowds. His immutable face, his arrogance, and his very long sermons (especially on the topic of offering) resulted in smaller attendances. Mesmer was also an arrogant and highly egocentric man. Randi also had the habit of kissing men on the cheek when he greeted them. Judas did the same to Jesus!

Friends of ours, who had moved all the way from Alaska to sit under Benny's anoint"Hinn"g, introduced us to the Lechner's ministry.

We still attempted to set a date for the appointment with Benny. This stupid situation, caused entirely by Benny's irresponsibility, had us going through emotional states that made every member of the family feel very insecure and very uncertain about the future. We felt useless and worthless.

So when our Alaskan friends told us about the prophets, we felt we needed to go. Perhaps we could hear from God. Those highly recommended prophets appeared to be the solution to our problems, to provide answers to our questions for we wondered about our situation.

The first meeting we attended took place on September 22, 1992. It was conducted by Cathy. She played piano and led us into some songs. Then she preached. After her sermon she said, "Anybody who wants to receive a prophecy, come to the front now." So the four of us walked up front. To Melanie, Nicole, and myself she said nothing too specific; although her method of operation impressed us. To Stephan, however, she had more to say:

> ...I believe that I hear from God and I speak the word of the Lord. I see through a glass darkly and I may not get all of it, but I heard the Lord say: overseas, overseas. God's gonna send you back to your people, I heard God say...."

We should have started questioning that ministry then. But we did not. For she said, "I see through a glass darkly and I may not get all of it." Why would the Lord give you a word if you cannot clearly see it? It doesn't make any sense. Then she said, "I heard the Lord say: overseas, overseas. God's gonna send you back to your people." Our people are Canadians, just north of the American border. Not overseas! But it thrilled us so much that we accepted the whole speech. We had been victimized by her mesmeric spell.

At the conclusion of the meeting we decided to talk to her. We were happy and excited. We told her that we were not accustomed to this, and that her ministry impressed us. My wife and I further explained our desire to proclaim the gospel worldwide. What a mistake we made of opening our heart to her!

But we accepted her prophecies and all the many others that followed as coming from God, and we hung on to them like a dying person hangs on to their last breath. We were assured that those prophecies originated from heaven. How gullible we were!

If I could compare it, I would say it is similar to a doctor you trust who, without telling you exactly what it is, injects you with a virus at your first visit—a virus that forces you to come back. And every time you visit your doctor, he gives you another shot of that same virus. We were strangers to the fact that prophecies from such people were nothing more than mesmerism. Such prophecies put your life under a spell, and until the day you realize it, your life is in a mess, and the enchantment gains force and strength over your will. Their prophecies are like a poison that infiltrates your veins and kills you slowly.

Consequently we went back to Cathy's meeting two weeks later. And she exercised the same modus operandi. After the praise and worship, the preaching and the offering, she told the congregation that if we needed a prophecy we had to go up front.

We hungered so much for another prophecy, and were so confident it originated from God, that we proceeded to the front like several others. Cathy came and addressed my family. She first gave a prophecy to Nicole and me. That day her prophecies were much more extensive. I will therefore summarize what she said:

> For the Lord says: it was I who plucked you up and moved you. It was I that relocated and replanted you. I don't know, I remember seeing your face but I don't remember anything about you [she says!].... For the Lord says: I will send you with and by the man of God...you shall interpret....

It can be easy to determine that a French-speaking translator, now living in Orlando, can interpret a man of God. But the context in general was quite impressive. At that moment, we could not really analyze such words. For us, this prophecy confirmed that we had to pursue our attempts to meet Benny Hinn. Surely he was the man of God. It all made sense. Then she walked to Melanie, asked her name, and said:

> Melanie, and I heard the Lord say and Melanie: this is where you will find the man of God. This is where you will find the man of God, says the Spirit of the Lord. How old are you? Hallelujah, 18! Well you can wait a couple of years, God. But anyway, but I heard the Lord say: it's in this place, it's in this place, in this area. God has got the man of God...

If their prophecies were inspired by the Spirit of God, why is Cathy surprised by Melanie's relatively young age? And why does she immediately say to God that he can wait a couple of years? She seems to certify that the event is about to take place. And when she adds, "But anyway," she seems to be resigned to the fact that Melanie will meet the man of God soon in spite of her young age.

Well, Melanie surely found a man in Orlando who feigned to be a man of God. He was a minister and crusade coordinator working in Asia for a dozen of the largest Christian ministries based in the United States. This man, however, came straight from the pits of hell. You will learn in Chapter Nine how this prophecy deceived and misled us. This prophecy devastated us.

Mesmerist Charles Poyen, who widely exercised in the United States, reported that roughly ten percent of his entranced subjects attained the "highest degree" of the magnetic condition. Reports of subjects performing feats of clairvoyance and extrasensory perception under this extraordinary state were not uncommon. The subjects could describe events transpiring in remote areas, and could read the minds of persons in the audience.[2] Mesmer's discoveries were passed down to Charles Poyen through the Marquis de Puységur. The Marquis de Puységur, Mesmer's most capable disciple, became Poyen's mentor. Bill Hamon's discoveries have been passed down to, among others, Randi Lechner. Randi, being Cathy's mentor, has injected his spirit in to her. And the mesmeric tradition continues.

The fruits those prophecies propagate are venomous and deadly. Their prophecies if they truly reveal, and I stipulate if they truly reveal anything that might be true, it is only manifested by divination.

These prophets, just like the faith healers, are very capable persons in their field. They are particularly strong in diagnosing the needs and wishes of the crowd. They are fake and dangerous people because, like the faith healers, they proclaim things in the name of God. And the prophecies, if they come to pass, only serve to put you in deeper distress.

What you trust to be really flowing from heaven is nothing less than an occult ritual that induce you into snares. Those prophets are not prophets of God as they claim to be. But at the time we ignored it. I cannot believe that we followed Machiavellian liars.

So whatever prophecy we received, emanating supposedly from the Spirit of God, we believed it. We unintentionally started to shape our lives in relation with the prophecies and to dream about their accomplishment. Do you realize the danger that dwells in listening to and believing such prophets?

We also attended a prophetic meeting on October 13, 1992. This time, Randi Lechner led the meeting. He operates like Cathy but with some differences. First, we did not sing at Randi's meetings; instead, we were told to bawl. And until the shouting reached a certain level of decibel, Randi ordered us to pray louder and louder. As if God was deaf! I need to mention that in the room next to the one we occupied, other meetings took place. And some staff members of the Civic Center also worked in their office. I wonder now what they thought about us.

Randi also told us that if we had any chain or bondage, they would fall if we jumped and danced. We did not feel comfortable at all with the yelling, or with the jumping and the dancing; so we refrained from doing so. Every time Randi turned his head in our direction and saw our attitude, he gave us a dirty look. If the eyes are the mirror of the soul, I can only imagine the condition of his soul.

After the shouting and the dancing, Randi preached, and preached, and preached. When he had completed his sermon, he started a very long exhortation on the offering. Everyone in the meeting was very tired. There is an old saying which says that when your bottom gets tired, so does your mind. After his exhortations and the gathering of the offerings, Randi, contrary to his wife, picked people in the audience asking them if he could prophesy over them.

Guess what? He had a prophecy for Nicole and me. He said that the opportunities of ministry would come from the left and the right, and that the Lord was breaking us loose from some hindrances. He added that the Lord would take us back in areas where promises had been made but not fulfilled. He finished his prophecy by saying that the Lord would roll a reproach off of us.

This prophecy seemed at that time factual and true because Benny had made a promise to us. And according to the prophecy, God said he would take us back to where the promises had been made, that is, OCC. Also we had come to believe that our reputation had been tarnished; thus, keeping us away from Benny just like in the case of Kenny Smith. Therefore, a reproach on our name needed to be taken off. At that moment we really started to believe in those guys. Even though nothing had happened, we still thought God had talked through these prophets. We thought that we just needed to be patient.

When you receive a prophetic word, Randi and Cathy advise you to get the tape, to write your prophecy down, pray over it, and to take it to your pastor (this way they publicize their ministry, thus opening doors for future invitations). In the Bible, prophecies coming from God required no special action on the part of the receiver. It came to pass no matter what. The Lechner's prophecies affect you like sleeping pills; they do not put you to sleep suddenly, but the doze gets you gradually.

This word gave me more motivation to try and reach Benny's secretary. So we kept on trying, and trying, and trying. Except that we still could not get an answer from Nancy.

We were hooked on those prophecies. The next time Cathy held a meeting in town we made a point of honor to attend it. Cathy prophesied to Nicole in a different way this time. She sang it.

In this one, the message was that my wife and I would have a ministry, and exhorted us to hang on; that it would take just a little bit longer for things to happen. This message energized our patience. But by this time Cathy knew about our precarious situation, and that we were still waiting for our immigration papers. Without these working permits no one could work; and without work, there was no income. It resulted in poverty and frustrations. Cathy utilized what she knew about our situation to give the word to Nicole.

Their workmanship and skills are nothing more than psychology, joined to a great capacity by the behavior of people, and backed up by a very good memory. The main point of their ministry, however, resides in the fact that they are driven by a spirit of divination, also known as mesmerism.

So we hung in there believing that Benny would, as he promised, help us. After all, the prophets confirmed it by their prophecies. Thus, filled with hope, we continued going to OCC. And I maintained my attempts to get in touch with Nancy.

These soothsayers tell their followers beautiful bedtime stories. If you believe their predictions, you will see your future as to a rose garden. For instance, almost every single who attends their meetings is prophesied a marriage. I assure you that their words mislead individuals—many who are eager to get married—to enter into relationships that should have been avoided. This reveals that they are not from God.

I just cannot find words to describe that kind of pretentious prophets. Their filthy words ruin people's lives by enticing them into deep troubles.

On March 4, 1993, Cathy gave another prophecy to Nicole and me. At the end she said, "And you shall have great celebration and rejoicing this year, says the Lord." She meant the year 1993 which proved to be, as you discover in the book, one of the toughest years of our lives. The year 1993 represents the year we suffered the most individually and as a family.

Let me relate few examples of illusory prophecies given to persons we knew personally.

The first one relates to a girl in her early twenties. She was prophesied that she would never lack money. Every time she would struggle financially, someone would show up and give her money. One evening, while Stephan was conversing with her, that girl confessed that she had the habit of spending her pay checks on clothes. And this unhealthy behavior caused her to be hungry, for she had no money left to buy groceries. She agreed with the word and kept her bad habit. A righteous prophet would have rebuked her.

Another young lady, whom we knew very well, got prophesied that she would get married. Well, this young lady was determined to get a specific young man to marry her—a life goal not shared by the poor fellow. He, too, attended OCC. A few weeks later in the church parking lot he confided, "You know Stephan, I really didn't like her, but now...I like her." He did not sound deeply convinced; Stephan could feel his misery. The poor fellow felt obliged to marry her because he believed the girl's argument. She used the prophecy to her advantage.

Two sisters in their early twenties and their mother never miss a prophetic meeting. None of them had a job and they were never exhorted by the prophets to find one. One sister even had a medical college degree, but she waited for an evangelist to fulfill her desire for a prophecy of marriage. What a pity to see them waiting for the fulfillment of their false prophecies—prophecies that were misleading them.

And it made us sick to our stomach to see people that could, but would not work, while we hoped every day for an answer from the résumés we had sent, from the green card lottery, or from Benny's promises. A positive answer would have given us our working permits and would have allowed us to be useful to the society. Every day we would check our mailbox and our answering machine for a message that would confirm our hopes that this would be The Day. Those were frustrating moments.

The more prophecies we received, the more confused and disorganized we became. In many instances during those eighteen months or so, we tried to meet Cathy and Randi outside their meetings. We desperately needed some explanations about the prophecies—prophecies that were not coming to pass. But neither of them could find the time to see us! Like all the other charlatans they have no desire or intention to face the people whom they have deceived. When you question their credibility and doubt the accuracy of their prophecies, they tell you to put the word you got on a shelf and wait for its coming. This is an easy way of getting out of trouble.

Stephan even faxed a letter, telling Randi that he was willing and ready to help him in the ministry. Randi did not even bother to acknowledge Stephan's letter.

Weeks later in a prophetic conference, Randi said to Stephan that he had been touched by the letter (I guess not touched enough to reply) and that he would contact him soon. After the discussion Randi gave Stephan the Judas kiss on the cheek! Well, Randi never fulfilled his word. He never contacted Stephan.

Those prophecies that we believed were coming from God undermined us as much as the disgusting behavior of Benny Hinn. Of course, these prophets and Benny operate in the same mesmeric field. We had yet to realize all the harm those devilish people were causing us.

We finally realized in 1994 that those prophecies had kept us under bondage. We stopped believing in them, rejected them all, and went on with our lives. Now we have discovered the true face of those fake prophets.

CHAPTER EIGHT
"HINN"TEGRITY AND ITS SEQUELS

As the month of September passed by, I had not yet succeeded in reaching Benny's secretary. Perhaps it stood as a normal procedure to wait almost three months to get an appointment with Mr. Hinn!

Things were kind of rough. The fact that we could not get to Benny left us with a sentiment of frustration and of despair; but most of all we felt rejected. We could not understand why a well-known man like Benny could not respect his own commitment. What were the sordid reasons that could explain this cynical behavior?

We saw on Channel 55 (WACX-TV), a Christian TV station located in Orlando, and affiliated with TBN, that the station was holding a telethon during the month of September. Their guest list included good singers and well-known preachers. And of course the town hero Benny Hinn was part of it as the guest speaker on the Thursday night broadcast. The evangelical television system is just like the show business of Hollywood.

The studios were open to the public, so we decided to see how they operated a fund-raising telethon. Mainly though, it represented a unique opportunity to talk face to face with Benny Hinn. No one can get to him in his church, but this time he would be out of his environment. We could not miss it.

Channel 55 was founded and is owned and operated by Claude Bower and his wife Freida. The Bowers are always welcome to sit in the front rows of OCC. You see, birds of a feather flock together. It works this way in those circles: You scratch my back and I will scratch yours.

Aside from the television station, the Bowers are also involved in the distribution of health products such as vitamins and minerals. They utilize lots of air time during the telethons to promote those products; thus, getting money from people via two avenues. They collect money sent by the viewers to keep the station on the air, and also the money spent by the viewers to buy their products. They work it out this way.

Let us say they offer a package deal that includes a bottle of a mineral solution and a book on how to use the product, and the package deal is available for a donation of $50 to the television station. When a viewer sends in the money, the station gets the offering; the book author, who is a guest speaker at the telethon, gets a royalty on the book sales; and Claude Bower gets a percentage on the sale of the product.

We have spoken to the Bowers, and have seen them on a few occasions in public places. The smiles that they show on the camera strangely disappears behind the scenes, and are replaced by an arrogant and snobbish attitude. Well, it is easy to understand: We were not part of their "crowd."

We spent just about every weeknight at the telethon, and we would sit in the studio and watch the live broadcast of the show. Thursday finally came. They opened the studio doors at 6:00 P.M. but we arrived there at 3:00 P.M. We wanted to be sure to get the front row seats. This is not Benny's church!

The lobby was packed. So when they opened the doors we rushed to get the front row seats. Then we awaited for the arrival of the "great man." Claude Bower and his wife Freida hosted the telethon, and they kept telling the audience that Benny would arrive very soon. Of course, they wanted to make sure every viewer would stay tuned. You see, this way they build up the expectations and hopes of the viewers; thus, increasing their pledges.

Benny was scheduled to be on at 8:00 P.M., but as usual he did not show up on time. Just like movie stars, he longs to be expected and acclaimed. He finally arrived at 9:00 P.M., without his wife Suzanne, but with his entourage of bodyguards and some of his yes men. Benny loves to build a wall of protection around his himself. Suzanne and the children arrived later that night.

It seemed strange that on some occasions I have seen his children alone by themselves in the children's ministry hall without any supervision. We also saw two of Benny's daughters in a restaurant in Orlando escorted only by one lady, although it was past midnight. Benny pretends he has received death threats; then, why does he leave his children without any protection, or with just a babysitter?

The most talented TV preachers, those with illustrious visual charisma, inevitably end up with their own enormous ego. They are treated as special individuals whom God uses in extraordinary ways, and they are looked up to as special gifted humans. This is the public face they project.

Benny started preaching around 9:30 P.M. I do not need to tell you that he preached on giving. He said that he felt a special "anointing" for those who would give money that night. Benny and Claude (that sure sounds to me like Bonnie and Clyde!) reassured everybody that every single pledge would be prayed for. But people had to hurry, and send in their pledges.

I never thought that one could stop God's blessings when the program would end! They really like to fool people. The evening programs were replayed the following day, from early morning till 7:00 P.M.—the beginning of the next live broadcast. Therefore, you could watch a rerun the next day and hear the same urgent message!

Those who call in are offered a gift. Of course, the bigger the pledge, the bigger the gift. This is another way for the guests to make money. Let's say, for example, that Benny is invited to preach, and that for every pledge they receive, the station gives a copy of Benny's newest book. Those copies are bought by the television station. On every book that is given to a pledger, Benny gets a royalty from the publisher.

Pledges are recorded on a special form, then forwarded on camera to Claude and his guests so that they can mention on the air in, order of importance, the amount pledged, followed by the pledger's name.

Benny quoted some Scriptures, preaching mainly to motivate people to send in money. He said that if people wanted to keep on seeing his programs on the station they had to hurry in their pledge; because without these donations to the telethon, the station would be unable to keep its doors opened. What an arrogant statement! Life goes on even without Benny on the air.

Benny explained the special anointing he felt coming from God. When Benny would lay hands on the copies of the pledges, everyone who had sent money to the telethon would receive his financial breakthrough. Any financial bondage people were under would be lifted if they sent money that night. Benny's special "anointing" would set them free from their debts that same night.

In a nation where there are scores of spiritually, medically, and financially deprived people, some TV programs fraudulently offer the possibility of possessing victory over practically any distress. Most of televangelism is similar to a religious version of the lottery window—it is somewhere to turn to when all other sources of expectation have presumably turned onto disenchantment.

And they say they are not in it for money!

After Benny's Oscar-winning performance, they stopped for a station break. A couple sitting behind Stephan called Benny regarding his next tour to Israel. So he, recognizing the couple that had traveled with him in the past, walked off the stage and came to shake hands with them. In doing so, he walked right by Stephan.

My wife immediately said to Stephan, "Grab a hold of Benny."

So he grabbed Benny's arm and asked, "What about our appointment, Pastor Benny?"

While gently tapping on Stephan's arm, he answered, "In God's timing, in God's timing."

Then Benny came in our direction. He came to me first. So I asked him, "What about our appointment, Pastor Benny? I have left many, many messages with your secretary over the last three months, and she has not called me back yet."

I also told him, "My French translation you requested of your book *Good Morning, Holy Spirit* is complete. Would you like to read it?"

He responded, "Sure." For he is able to read French. He kept on walking and shook hands with Nicole and Melanie after which he walked back towards the stage. At this moment Melanie addressed him, "Pastor Benny! You have not made a promise in front of a man, you have made a promise in front of God."

He turned back towards her and exclaimed, "What?" His complexion had turned from natural to ghostly white.

For the first time, I saw some fear in his face—the same type of fear I would later see in the national *Inside Edition* exposé.

She repeated the same thing, "You have not made a promise in front of a man but in front of God."

And she added, "And God is my friend and I talk to him about you and about the promises you have made but not respected."

Benny replied, "You're a tough lady. Give your phone number to Kent Mattox. He'll call you."

Within the next few seconds I wrote our names and phone number and gave it to Kent Mattox. Now the ball was in their court. We did not know it would turn into a sting because Benny failed that night to tell us, face to face, that he had no intention of fulfilling his promises.

Kent Mattox is the jack-of-all-trades of Benny Hinn. He is also very, very close to him. Benny has told his congregation that Mattox is his confident, and added that he knew more things on Benny than anybody else. Did he even know more than Benny's wife?

For example Mattox, and Mattox alone, is allowed during the crusades to go and tell Benny that the time has come to get ready and go on stage to perform his act. Benny does not tolerate anyone else, not even a member of his family.

I remember one incident in church. Mattox was sitting in the first pew, and Dave Palmquist was sitting on the platform right next to Benny. The "great man" demanded that Palmquist change places—Benny needed to have Mattox close to him. Mattox is also the only member of the pastoral staff who chaperones Benny on vacation. If Benny goes to TBN, Mattox goes with him; if Benny goes to Israel, Mattox goes with him; if Benny goes to the restroom, well, I am not sure if Mattox....

Benny Hinn, Kent Mattox, Gene Polino, and the bodyguards travel luxuriously. Benny flies first class, stays in first-class hotels, and eats first-class meals. Let me put it to you in plain words: Those first-class expenses are paid for by all the people that give money in the form of tithes, offerings, or special donations to Benny Hinn's ministry. Those people expect this money to be spent for the kingdom of God, not for men's capricious desires.

And they say they are not in it for money!

The telethon was over, but our hopes were riding high. The "great man" had us hooked once again. He had told us to give our phone number to his right hand man Kent Mattox, which we did, and we still believed that things could happen. Benny had also accepted my invitation to read my translation of *Good Morning, Holy Spirit*.

So the next day I went to the church's receptionist desk and gave my translation to the lady, telling her to make sure that the package was given to Pastor Benny Hinn himself. The same day Suzanne Hinn saw the package, inquired about it, took it and gave it to Curtis—one of Benny's faithful bodyguards. Suzanne ordered Curtis to make sure that her husband got the envelope in his hands. I know how it happened because a lady friend of ours accompanied Suzanne that day. This lady later related the facts.

Pastor Fred Spring asked us to do some volunteer work on the church prayer line. The church leadership finds the time to entrust us with that kind of responsibility, but it finds no time to meet and to pay us. What a wonderful way to get cheap labor!

Like all big Christian ministries, this one has its own prayer lines where people in need of prayers call, of course, at their own expense. The lines are opened to the public from morning till evening. Night callers can leave a message on the voice mail. The phone calls are returned collect because Benny's ministry does not want to pay long-distance charges pertaining to the prayer ministry. During our volunteer work, the ministry leader got excited because the prospect of having a toll-free 800 number had been presented to the administration. Her excitement was short-lived. The idea was rejected by Gene Polino.

We volunteered three afternoons a week from 1:00 P.M. till 4:00 P.M. You would not believe all the phone calls this ministry receives from all over the world.

This ministry, because of its outreach, produces a strong impact on people, and therefore brings in its share of revenues. But its workers, except for the leader, are all volunteers. But located in the same trailer are the paid personnel responsible for handling the reservations of buses coming to the crusades. Could it be that Polino and Benny consider the work of the prayer line personnel not worthy of being on the payroll?

A lot of followers choose to write rather than call. They send a letter detailing all their prayer needs, and include in most cases some cash, or a money order, or a check.

It worked out as follows: When letters requiring prayers arrived on the premises, they were dispatched to the prayer line ministry. We have seen the leader open envelopes, remove the donation, put the envelopes in stacks, and place them in box in a corner of the office. Thus, it was possible that a written prayer request could have been prayed for many weeks after its arrival. And if their request needed an immediate answer, well, they should have called. How is that for first-class efficiency, Mr. Hinn!

We volunteered at the prayer line ministry for almost four months. Stephan, Melanie, and I answered the phone. My wife Nicole interceded individually for the requests that came in through the mail or by phone. Others also answered the phone, but we never witnessed anyone else interceding for the requests in the box. Pastor Fred should have taken the stacks and distributed the prayer request forms in his morning prayer meetings, instead of telling his boring stories. This way the meetings would have fulfilled their purpose.

In that period we were still awaiting the phone call from Mattox. I believe he attended the same school as Benny's secretary, a school where they did not teach elementary manners and respect for human beings.

We then began to raise serious doubts about his staff. We thought that Benny really wanted to meet us, but that some influential members close to him had successfully raised barriers. We still hoped that Benny would, one way or another, remember our appointment.

November was at our doorstep, and we would celebrate our first Thanksgiving Day in the United States. Christopher and Karen Hinn invited us for Thanksgiving dinner. Their hospitality was appreciated, and their dinner very good. I had the occasion to talk to Christopher about our moving experience, about my translation of Benny's book, and about the promise his brother had made to us. He said he would talk to him and straighten out the matter. He also added that the next time Benny went go to Europe, I would accompany him. That evening we also met Mamma Hinn and the youngest son of the family, Michael.

Karen told us that four years earlier they owned almost nothing. But they now live in a very luxurious house, drive three vehicles; they are living the high lifestyle. The reason for that monetary improvement is the travel agency Christopher owns and operates. Benny and his staff who do a lot of traveling are one, if not the principal, first-class customers of Christopher's agency. Aside from the Mercedez-Benz car Christopher drives, and the Chrysler Town and Country van that his wife uses to drive the kids around, Karen is also the owner of a Porsche 911 car.

Here is the true story Karen related to us about the Porsche. Karen said, "I made a deal with Chris. I told him: I'll give you three children, then you give me a Porsche." Chris agreed. After the three children, Karen got the Porsche.

Karen mentioned so many things about the Hinn family that she, after a while, repeatedly incited us to return to Canada for good. She felt pressure, and saw us as witnesses and threats after her negative comments.

One day Christopher called me. He inquired about the fact that I supposedly wanted to sue OCC for losing a scarf that I had given them four months earlier. Allow me to explain.

A friend of ours living in Montreal, who was at that time very sick, sent her favorite scarf to my attention in Orlando. She wanted me to ask Benny Hinn to pray over her scarf, and afterwards to send it back to her. She believed that her scarf—after being prayed over by the "great man"—would have a healing effect on her sickness. After all, faith healers teach that an action is required from the part of the subject. They say it is a step of faith. Some call it a "point of contact."

So upon receiving the parcel, I took the envelope bearing our friend's name and containing the scarf to the church and gave it to Bonnie, the lady responsible for the front rows in the church. I explained to her the nature of the request and asked her to give it to Benny, since she had access to his office. I believe she took the scarf to Benny's office.

The following Sunday I asked Bonnie if we could recover it. She went backstage to find it, but the scarf could not be located. No one could find it. Finally Bonnie told me that the famous scarf landed in Benny's home. I still do not know how.

We never got the scarf back. So we took for granted that it was lost. That loss caused our friend in Montreal a lot of grief.

Then unexpectedly, four months later, Christopher asked that strange question, "Is it true, Yves, that you want to sue the church for a scarf that has been lost?"

I answered him that I had no intention in suing the church. I added that it would cost me more in suing the church, then in buying our friend a new scarf! That story was preposterous. Whoever came up with this idea had the intention of attacking our reputation. They purposely forged a story as in the case of Kenny Smith. And similarly, we could not plead our case face to face with Benny.

Christopher called me again in December because his brother Henry—who pastors a church in Vancouver, Canada—was planning to hold a crusade in Montreal in the month of March, 1993. He wanted to know if I would give Henry a hand in obtaining some contacts. I accepted because we still had many good contacts in our hometown. I realized later that it did not matter if it involved Henry, Benny, or Christopher; once you have known one, you have known the three. I will elaborate on the integrity of Henry in Chapter Twelve.

Allow me tell you about a little incident that occurred during the 1992 OCC Christmas party to which they invited Henry Hinn. To entertain the people, some members of the staff produced a video on the Hinn family. I am not aware of what they showed on that tape, but Henry himself told us about the incident.

He said, "After I watched the tape, I got real mad and ran after Gene Polino. I grabbed him by his tie, and cursed him." Henry felt that some sequences of the videotape insulted his family. This is a very strange reaction from a man who never misses an occasion on the platform to make fun of his older brother Benny.

The fact that we could not get our appointment with Benny, thus delaying us from getting our working permits, plus the highly expected but unknown results of the green card lottery had put our finances in a precarious situation. Stephan and I had sent more then 150 résumés to various firms in Orlando and the area, but nothing concrete had come out of these quests for work.

The year 1993 stood at our doorstep, and the church held a New Year's Eve service. We attended the service because it gave us an occasion to extend to our friends and acquaintances our best wishes for the New Year. And of course Benny utilized that service to utter some of his "astonishing" prophecies for the coming year. Benny affirmed under the "anointing" that God would visit the United States and President Bill Clinton in 1993.

Yes Benny is also a fake prophet. One of his close friends confided to me that Benny uses his false prophecies to settle his internal business on stage. For example, when Benny prophesied to Pastor Palmquist that he would be in charge of the partners, this matter had already been settled behind the scenes. Benny, however, used the church platform to make it look like a prophetic word from God.

The other subjects he mentioned were more sweet talk than prophecies. He added that God would give us a divine memory. Those exhortations were given in a general context, so they applied to Benny as well as to anyone else in the church. I have to believe that God did not give Benny a divine memory. Even in 1993 he forgot about our appointment!

CHAPTER NINE
ON ROAD TO SINGAPORE

In the week of January 4-8, 1993, Morris Cerullo held his 22nd Annual World Conference at the Marriott's Orlando World Center in Florida. The list of guest speakers included, just to name a few, R.W. Schambach, Roberts Liardon, Ed Cole, Tim Storey, and the local star Benny Hinn; and of course, the host of the conference Morris Cerullo—better known in the Christian inner circles as M.C. We call him the "push-button weeping puppet."

Morris Cerullo is a renowned evangelist. He launched his Morris Cerullo World Evangelism ministry in 1961, with the headquarters based in San Diego, California. His wife Theresa takes also part in the ministry but only to project a family image. Theresa does not attend any planning meetings, for Morris is against the presence of women in important meetings. Morris uses his wife as a decoy.

The Assemblies of God ordained Morris Cerullo as a minister in 1952. In the early 1950s, while attending a local Assembly of God church, Cerullo prophesied that God called him to a special work. Six months later, he had a vision that convinced him of his calling into the ministry with a worldwide emphasis. He also felt a calling to present the Christian message to every Jew on earth before the return of Christ.

In the early years of his ministry, he was associated with William Marrion Branham, a preacher who lived a very questionable life. Indeed, Branham came to believe he was the apocalyptic prophet messenger. This "prophet" emphasized healing in his evangelical work. Faith healing also became an emphasis in Cerullo's ministry. After ministering for many years in Europe, Asia, and Africa, where he added his schools of ministry—a training school targeting indigenous church leaders—he commenced in 1970 a new priority in his ministry on the North American continent. He has since spent his evangelical efforts in America as well as overseas.

We had a dual purpose in attending Cerullo's World Conference. First, it would enable us to see in person ministers that we could only see on television; and second it created a great opportunity for me—a translator—to make contact with them.

Some fees had to be paid for the conference, but for the residents of the Orlando area, no charges applied. I must say that Cerullo, for the first time since 1972, held his conference outside of California. And he selected Orlando, where we had just moved.

Early Monday morning we drove to the Marriott's Resort—one of the nicest and most expensive resorts of the region—because the thousands of participants in the conference had to register early. After the registration, we sat in one of the numerous lobbies of the hotel awaiting the night service.

While we were waiting, I felt led to talk to Cerullo's people about my translation work. I met Connie Broom and had a very interesting conversation with her. She is the editor responsible for all of Morris Cerullo's books and literature. She seemed very interested in my work and asked me to write to her the following week at their office in San Diego.

Then it was time for the evening service. The host, the unique Morris Cerullo, opened the conference that Monday night. I have never been impressed by Cerullo's way of preaching. I just cannot stand preachers who feel the necessity of yelling and the urge of crying to get their message through. Only professional actors can willingly cry in any circumstances, and Cerullo is certainly one of them. But tears rarely come out of his eyes.

The next day of the conference the guest preacher was R.W. Schambach. I have to tell you how these guys operate, especially in a full house. Schambach said that he felt led to do something "special." So he asked for 1,000 people who would make a pledge of a $1,000 each. He felt the urge of supporting financially such a good work—meaning Cerullo's ministry.

R.W. Schambach is the same preacher who credited A.A. Allen—a famed faith healer—for the earthquake that struck the California city of Eureka, and the flood which damaged the same city in December, 1955. Schambach claimed these events happened because the A.A. Allen ministry had been denied the use of Eureka municipal auditorium![1]

It is a well-known fact behind the scenes that every time Morris Cerullo organizes a conference or a crusade, most if not all the expenses are covered in advance, most of the time by the mailing list partners. In spite of that, in response to Schambach's request, between 1,000 and 1,500 people agreed to give $1,000.

Now if you make a basic calculation, you end up with one to one million five hundred thousand dollars. And that represents only the Tuesday morning "special" offering, not the "regular" offerings they took every meeting.

And they say they are not in it for money!

Because I had been prophesied by the Lechners that we would make contacts, we all made a special effort to talk to the guest speakers. Proceeding as our own public relations agent, we started asking almost every one of them if they needed a translator.

On Tuesday, while Melanie walked in the hotel lobby, she met a man who said he lived in Malaysia. He also declared to our daughter that he was the right-hand man of Morris Cerullo in Asia.

He introduced himself as Raymond Mooi, the founder of A.C.T.S. Global Networking in Malaysia. A.C.T.S means Asian Christian Training School, a school for ministers in Asia. Mooi stands, indeed, very close to Morris Cerullo. Mooi acted very charmingly and very respectfully with our daughter.

The following day, he gave us passes that allowed all the family to have breakfast and lunch at the hotel that day. Those passes were normally given to the persons who had paid to attend the conference, but he said that they would be wasted if we did not use them. We welcomed them because it saved us a lot of money, and the hotel served very good quality meals.

On Wednesday we attended the morning, afternoon, and night meetings. They held three meetings a day, in addition to the early morning prayer meeting. During one prayer meeting, Raymond prayed on stage with extreme fervency, and we were quite impressed because he looked so devout. His sanctimonious appearance deceived us.

We met Raymond Mooi once again. He acted with very charming and gallant manners toward Melanie. Since he knew that I was a translator, he proved, by managing an appointment between us and Roberts Liardon, that he kept very good relations with these preachers. We met Roberts in his hotel room, and he gave us the name and phone number of his publishing manager, although he promised nothing.

Let me explain why his name is Roberts, and not simply Robert. His mother, being the first student to give birth while she studied at Oral Roberts University, named him Roberts. I wonder how she would have named him if she had studied at UCLA, or at Harvard!

Melanie mentioned to us that Raymond had inquired about her marital status. She told him that she was single; then in return Melanie asked Raymond the same question. He replied with the same answer. Those guys are like serpents, charming serpents.

Guest speakers preached in the morning and afternoon, while Morris Cerullo, the "push-button weeping puppet," reserved the evening sessions for himself. Morris made an exception Thursday night for his good friend Benny.

That night featured the local star Benny Hinn. The "great man" asked if he could have his church choir sing at the meeting. Nobody dared to refuse him such a favor. So the choir, its director, the church pianist, and even the church organist were asked to participate in the meeting. Benny needed his mesmeric atmosphere.

The attendance for the conference averaged six thousand people; but for that special "Healing Service" they had to rent another ballroom adjacent to the regular one. Benny Hinn is really a crowd pleaser. Melanie, who sang in the OCC choir, took part in that special service.

A very strange thing occurred while Benny was preaching in the main ballroom. My wife and I attended the meeting in the adjacent room, and we saw to our great surprise, just a few tables away from us, Gene Polino. While Benny was giving the longing crowd his habitual "anointed" performance, Gene Polino, the church's administrator, rested sound asleep in his chair. Perhaps he was mesmerized by the anoint"Hinn"g!

After the service Raymond, accompanied by his right-hand man Alfred, invited us to the restaurant. He said that it would be an opportunity to know each other better. They gave us a good impression.

Then came Friday, the final day of the conference. There is a well-established custom that on the last day of those Annual World Conferences, Morris Cerullo anoints people with oil. So that day they set people in lines, and Cerullo, with Raymond standing beside him, walked and laid hands on everyone, which meant about six thousand people that day. The majority fell down under Cerullo's mesmeric power.

Mesmerist Charles Poyen, just like his French mentor Puységur, strongly believed in the mesmeric sleep. He therefore conducted his public lectures around the demonstration of this state which is like today's phenomenon of falling under "God's power." Poyen would succeed, with his manual gestures, in putting the majority of the volunteers into the mesmeric sleep. They would then awake and pretend to remembering nothing of what had transpired. It seems easy to induce the mesmeric trance. The phenomenon is now becoming common in the faith healing circles. People who fall down often declare that they do not remember anything.

After the meeting, Raymond told Melanie that he had postponed his departure to California to spend an extra day in our company. So we invited him to come to our home and have dinner with us. He accepted. We felt that something was going on between Melanie and Raymond (for they enjoyed one another's company). Now, remember that Melanie had been "prophesied" that she would meet the man of God in Orlando. And that is in addition to my prophecy, "You're gonna make contacts."

We invited Raymond back on Saturday to have lunch with us, just before his departure. Again he accepted. The same night he called us and asked to talk to Melanie. They must have spent over an hour on the phone.

During his trip the TBN network leadership invited Raymond to appear as a guest on "Praise the Lord." The program was hosted that night by Carlton Pearson—a well-known preacher. Needless to say, we watched the telecast. We even taped it. Every day and every night of that week, Raymond called Melanie. He called our home after attending meetings with Morris in San Diego, and he also called from John Avanzini's office in Colleyville, Texas.

On Friday, January 15, Morris Cerullo invited Raymond to preach at the staff prayer meeting held in the headquarters chapel. When Cerullo introduced him to his staff, he said that he loved the man like he loved his own son, adding that Raymond was the closest person to him on earth—a tactful statement for his family. And Morris even took an offering for him. Raymond collected over $5,000 from this visit.

Raymond shared with Melanie his desire to come back to Orlando on Saturday, January 16. He also informed her that John Avanzini wanted me to translate five of his books. Finally doors were opening for us, just as the prophecies had stated it!

On Saturday afternoon we drove to the airport to greet him. Raymond said he could stay only a few days, for he needed to return to Texas the following week. He had picked out the first two books John Avanzini wanted me to translate. We had to hurry because Raymond needed to leave for Asia February 1st, and the books had to be translated before his departure. So we rented a computer, and Stephan and I did the impossible— we translated two books in two weeks. It represented fifteen to sixteen hours of work a day, non-stop.

Things were getting very serious between Melanie and Raymond. I thought, "At last some of our prophecies are coming to pass. Melanie has met the man of God, and I have made successful contacts." Finally, we had reasons to rejoice. It had been seven long exhausting months since Benny's promises.

Raymond departed for Texas, and again he called us every day. Melanie enjoyed receiving long phone calls from him. Raymond came back to Orlando, Saturday 23. We went to greet him at the airport, and while we awaited his arrival, guess who came out of the plane? Benny Hinn himself and his usual entourage—Polino, Mattox, and some bodyguards.

Benny knew Raymond, because during the flight from Dallas to Orlando, Benny, Polino, and Raymond had talked about the possibility of organizing some crusades in Asia. They had also invited him to OCC for the upcoming Sunday service.

Raymond accepted the invitation, and we accompanied him to the church. During the service, Benny greeted Raymond and asked him to stand. We were all sitting in the front rows with the "in crowd." I remember that during the service Benny kept looking at us with an angry look on his face. He probably knew the true story about Raymond but, as usual, Benny chose to avoid the problem instead of facing it and finding solutions to it. You are a real first-class pastor, Mr. Benny!

During Raymond's stay in Orlando we got to know him better. Besides the week-long conference and the several days during his first trip, he had being spending more time with Melanie and our family. That particular week amounted to a very busy one, to say the least. First we needed to complete the translation of the two books; second Raymond said that he wanted to talk to us.

He told stories of his childhood; talking about the lady who adopted and raised him in a Buddhist temple, and the girl he later met. He did not love the girl but, since they unexpectedly had sexual intercourse, he felt the obligation to marry her. So he did, but it resulted in an unhappy marriage. Now that he was a preacher, his wife would not help him in the ministry. For instance she would sit in the back of the church while he would preach, and she would not even allow him to declare publicly their relationship and Christian faith.

For a period of time he even stopped his work with the various ministries just to please her. But he felt miserable and had lost his peace. He had to get back into it. Finally, she gave him the choice: her, or the ministry. He chose the ministry.

Consequently they broke up, and they had stopped living together. She had left him nine months earlier. Although he tried time and time again to reconcile with her, she stubbornly kept refusing. She was now living with her parents. The Moois have no children.

Obviously, Raymond supported his claims and story with a biblical text. He gave a passage in First Corinthians, Chapter 7—a chapter dealing with marriage principles. So he said, "But if the unbeliever departs, let him depart; a brother or a sister is not under bondage in such cases. But God has called us to peace" (1 Cor. 7:15).

He said, "For several years my marriage was going down the drain, and for the last nine months we have not lived together. I have never thought of getting remarried but since I met Melanie, and fell in love with her, I want to divorce my wife, and marry Melanie." He also added that he waited to tell us the truth because he feared he would lose Melanie's love.

We were very surprised by this revelation, but understood that he had made a mistake in marrying that girl. Surely God had forgiven him, and given him the chance to start anew. That is how he successfully tried to make us see it.

In addition, he said that all the big ministries he worked for knew his sad story, and that they even strongly suggested that he divorce her and start a new relationship. Men like Cerullo and Avanzini felt that Raymond's wife was not even saved, and that he needed a strong wife to support him in the ministry. He asked if could get engaged to Melanie before his departure for Asia. This great honor would give him strength and courage to advance to his next move, because a divorce is not easily obtained in Malaysia—an Islamic country. Raymond is really a serpent, an excellent lying serpent.

The biblical text he made use of to support his story, plus the Lechner's prophecies, plus the support received from several big Christian ministries convinced us of his sincerity. We had been treacherously deceived. The true face of Raymond Mooi eventually showed quite a different picture.

Melanie deeply loved Raymond, and it seemed he felt the same. We were sure that Melanie—as prophesied by Cathy—had found the man of God. So we agreed. Melanie and Raymond got engaged. The engagement took place on Monday, January 25, 1993, in a beautiful steamboat restaurant docked in Disney World.

We all shared Melanie's and Raymond's happiness. She was in love with him, and was persuaded that he was honest and truthful. We were convinced of his feelings towards Melanie. All of this came very suddenly, but we had the certainty that God was showing His will, because that is how the prophet had put it.

The next day, on Tuesday, we took Raymond to Randi Lechner's prophetic meeting. Before the meeting, Melanie and Raymond told him about their engagement.

Later that night, Randi gave a prophecy to Raymond telling him what a great "man of God" he was, and how God had put a great anointing on his life. He also added that Raymond would suffer a great rejection; that he would live in a country that is not one of his fathers; and that he would lose a family, but that God would give him another family.

That only reassured us of the direction we were taking. For in Malaysia—a Muslim country—divorced people are despised and even rejected by their families. It could also mean that Melanie and Raymond, once married would live in the United States or Canada. By divorcing, Raymond would lose his family, but with Melanie he would obtain a new one.

Of course none of those prophecies came to pass. Randi never raised any illegality or unethical behavior about the whole matter, like the engagement, despite Raymond's marital status. Randi did not even warn us of any upcoming tragedy. If he had been a prophet of God, he would have warned us against Raymond's real intentions. But as an oracle of the devil, and practioner of mesmerism, he covered the wicked one and misled the trustful. This reveals the fiendish nature of such flimflammers, and proves my exposé on faith healers and fake prophets.

After the service, we talked with Randi and gave him a few details on Raymond's involvements with big ministries. For that reason Randi asked Raymond to pray for him. He was in admiration, bowing before him. In our presence Randi had never asked any one of his followers to pray for him, and neither has he asked it since. For you see, Raymond had very close relations with big ministries, and big ministries meant big bucks. The possibility of getting close to those big guys impressed Randi—a very materialistic man. He was hypnotized by the possibility of huge benefits.

And they say they are not in it for money!

The next day came with its share of surprises. Raymond asked me if Melanie and Stephan could go with him to Asia. The trip would last between four and eight weeks, and they would not have to worry about the finances. Raymond wanted to bring them to Asia, because he claimed that Melanie and Stephan would be of a tremendous help in setting up crusades for about twelve large Christian ministries. Paying the children's expenses would be like paying their salary.

Mainly he wanted Melanie to know, before the marriage, the extent of his involvement in the ministry. He wanted to make sure that it would not hurt their relationship and stand against his ministry. He closed his speech saying, "This trip is important because I do not want to live another broken marriage."

They would organize crusades for ministers like R.W. Schambach, John Avanzini, Marilyn Hickey, Mike Evans, the singer Carman, Carlton Pearson, Roberts Liardon, Tim Storey, and of course Morris Cerullo. The money given by these wealthy ministries would pay their expenses. The money those ministries receive, however, is sent by innocent people in various monthly money donations.

Stephan would have the opportunity to help, and for Melanie, the dream continued. My wife and I would have never allowed Melanie to go alone with Raymond before their marriage; therefore he—realizing it—asked Stephan to be their chaperon. We accepted the offer. They would leave with Raymond on Monday, February 1, 1993.

That left us with a very short time to complete the translations, plus Stephan and Melanie had to get all their luggage ready. The departure day quickly arrived. The children were very excited about the whole thing. We naturally accompanied them to the airport, and kissed our children and wished all of them a safe trip. It never crossed our mind that we would not see Raymond Mooi again.

They first stopped in Los Angeles, California, then they drove to San Diego in order to meet Morris Cerullo and his wife Theresa. Upon their arrival at their San Diego headquarters, they were introduced as brother and sister to Morris, his wife Theresa, their daughter, and their now deceased son Mark, as well as several staff members.

Melanie wore her engagement ring during the entire visit. They especially spent time with Don Mandell—the right-hand man of Cerullo—organizing and planning the upcoming crusade in Hong Kong. None of them mentioned Mooi's wife in their presence, as if she did not exist. In two days nothing was said such as, "So how is your wife, Raymond?"

Raymond's sentimental attitude towards Melanie was plain to see. Morris saw Raymond putting his coat on her shoulders in the freezing TV studio, and Raymond kissing Melanie. So what excuse did they have for avoiding the subject of Raymond Mooi's marital situation?

They drove back to Los Angeles in order to fly to Hong Kong; and from there they flew to Singapore, Kuala Lumpur, and Bangkok. They wrote to us quite often, so we could follow them in their adventure.

While the children traveled in Asia, my wife and I woke up one morning only to realize that our car had disappeared. So I called the police department to report a stolen vehicle. But to our surprise and disappointment, the officer announced that our car had been repossessed. We were two car payments behind, but the company never advised us. They decided to take this radical action without a warning.

Without a car, and with bus service not being a priority in Orlando, we had to walk one to two miles to get to the nearest major store or mall. So on a daily basis, Nicole and I would make an habit of going out and taking our healthy walk. That surely kept us in very good shape. Aside from losing our car, we had another reason to be very sad. Our dog Boule, that we had adopted as a puppy nine years earlier, had to be put to sleep.

While the children journeyed in Asia, Boule got a very severe flea infection. Naturally we used shampoos, powders, collars. Even a pest control company came for treatments. And in spite of our prayers it brought no improvement. The infection was so severe that we had to take her to the veterinarian. She suffered constantly. She suffered so much so that she kept biting herself, to the point that rashes covered all her back, and the poor dog had lost a lot of hair.

After examining our dog the vet declared, "She has a very severe infection. I will have to make some tests, and give her antibiotics. But even then, I'm not sure it will save her life." He added that the cost of such a treatment averages $500. What could we do? We did not have that kind of money to spend on our dog. Only one solution remained: put Boule to sleep. We could not let her suffer anymore. That had to be one of the toughest decisions in our lives. Those who have pets know what it feels like.

So the next day we asked our friends from Alaska to come with us to the Humane Society. What a painful and sad decision we had to take, for we dearly loved our dog. The poor animal was so infected that her body released the smell of death.

Nicole and our friend stayed in the pickup truck. She did not have the courage to watch Boule go. So I took Boule to the clerk, filled out the form, and took Boule for her last walk. She did not even look back.

My wife and I cried a large portion of that day. What a painful way for a dog to end its life.

On the other side of the globe, Stephan, Melanie, and Raymond were traveling from one country to another. For the duration of their trip, they stayed in first-class hotels like the Westin Stamford, the Westin Plaza, the Imperial Queen's Park Hotel, and the Sukhotai Bangkok. They changed hotels every few days, not because of poor service, but because Raymond was running away from trouble. Rats always do. Of course, he did not tell Stephan and Melanie the true reason of those changes. The true reason was that Raymond's wife as well as some ministries were trying to locate him, but so far unsuccessfully.

Stephan and Melanie were taken to these luxurious places by Raymond himself. The Westin Stamford in Singapore, the tallest hotel in the world with its seventy three stories, and the Westin Plaza are classified as a superior first-class hotels. The Imperial Queen's Park Hotel in Bangkok, with its 1,400 rooms, charges $318 to $477 a night for a suite. The Sukhotai Bangkok, a sophisticated first-class hotel resort, charges for a suite $298 to $1193 a night![2] They certainly enjoyed their trip.

Why was it necessary for Raymond to sojourn in such luxurious places? I need to explain his lodging choices. I must say that he, as the crusade director for several fake preachers, did not end up in such luxurious hotels overnight. He just follows the regular recommendations of the ministries he works for—and those ministries obviously have very high standards.

It is attractive to lodge in a higher quality hotel when you are proposed to stay there without spending more than you would at a regular one. So why did the children accept? Simply because Raymond was lying about the room prices.

For instance, he said that at the Sukhotai Bangkok Resort he obtained a bargain from the sales manager—only $90 a night for the suite. When they checked out however, Stephan and Melanie found out that he paid three times as much! You should have seen the bill printout. That really upset them, because the money used to pay these bills comes from the ministry partners. You realize that it takes a lot of "$20 a month" to pay for such extravaganzas. No wonder they ask for $1,000 pledges in their meetings!

In many cities in which they stayed, Raymond was invited to preach; but he did not know until the last minute what verses he would speak on. Raymond, on Sunday mornings, does not have any breakfast and even refuses juice.

I have come across very interesting information. Buddhists, especially those trained in the priesthood, fast once a week, some on Sundays. I have to think that Raymond has not forsaken his Buddhist habits. He is probably the first Christian-Buddhist preacher! How is it that "anointed" men like Cerullo, Liardon, Avanzini and many others who work with him do not have the spiritual discernment to discover such a scary truth?

Of course the church where he would preach would take an offering for him. Melanie and Stephan were very surprised at the way Raymond spent money—money raised to help build God's kingdom.

Well Raymond, like his role models, utilizes a few tricks of his own to make money. He would, for example, make two or three photocopied sets of the hotel and flight receipts; and charge and collect them from two or three different ministries. I have to say that our children felt very uncomfortable with the way he behaved. They shared their disagreements with him, but he would always have a way out.

Raymond loved to gossip about the ministries he worked for. All those ministers, had in his eyes, all sorts of personal problems: immorality, fraud, greedy spirits, very high lifestyle, etc. The problem, however, is that by staying in this corrupt environment, he became just like them without seeing his own faults.

Those ministers shared one common feeling: they trusted him. So they paid him very good money. It was an investment for them because when they hold their crusades in Asia, they get tremendous money returns out of their campaigns. For instance, Raymond pioneered the work of American televangelists in Communist China. For this reason, they voluntarily ignored the fact that he cheated them. But when you cheat with other's people money, you cheat in every aspect of your life.

Raymond is also credited for having rescued Morris Cerullo in his purchase of Heritage USA. Let me explain. After the fall of PTL, Preacher Oral Roberts was interested in buying the complex. He shared his intentions with Cerullo who later turned back and bid higher (nice integrity). Struggling in raising the required $52 million, Cerullo asked his good friend Raymond to help him. So Raymond prepared a meeting with one of the richest man of Malaysia—a man who owns the whole Kentucky Fried Chicken chain in his country.

The man had no intention of meeting the "push-button weeping puppet," but thanks to Raymond, the introduction took place. Cerullo successfully convinced him to invest in the purchase of Heritage USA, which was at the time the third most frequented theme park in America. These insights were privately given by Raymond himself. The following is what the public knows.

The whole deal was settled and the conglomerate MUI became the majority shareholder. The relationship was short-lived. After they warned Cerullo several times about his promotional practices of selling Gold and Platinum Card memberships without their consent, and lawsuits were filed, they worked out an agreement whereby Cerullo surrendered his ownership to the majority shareholders. The details of that agreement were not made public.[3]

But we know, via the confidences of Raymond, that the deal made Cerullo and his organization eighteen million dollars richer; whereas the conglomerate MUI was losing $80,000 a month in the operation of their new acquisition.

During the trip, things were getting tougher for Mooi. Money was running low, time was running short. The walls were closing in on him. He had to make a move. And he did.

On Sunday, in Bangkok, Raymond claimed his wallet, containing all the money and all his IDs, had been stolen by a pickpocket. Luckily, they still had plane tickets to go to Cambodia. So they sold these tickets, and bought tickets to return to Singapore— where he pretended he had money in the bank. Upon their arrival he alleged that his wife had emptied the bank account.

He told Melanie and Stephan that he needed to quickly fly to Kuala Lumpur in order to get copies of his IDs, and that in his hometown he would get more money. He would leave on Monday morning, but said that he would come back the same night— because they wanted to return to the States on Tuesday.

While Raymond was packing some of his belongings, the children kept asking him why he was sorting various items. He pretended that they had too much luggage to enter the United States; thus, he would leave one trunk to the concierge's desk where a couple he knew would pick it up and bring it to Los Angeles. We later discovered that, mixed up in his lies, he even grabbed some of the children's clothing. He also took a sapphire-diamond bracelet he had given to Melanie—a bracelet he pretended he had lost during the journey.

Then came Monday night and Raymond had shown no sign of life. The children became very worried and barely slept because Melanie got very nervous thinking that an accident might have happened. They had no way of contacting him, so they called home. She shared her anxiety and kept on crying. Nicole and I could only try to comfort her and pray for them.

Tuesday morning, the children could not tolerate the anxiety. So they went to the hotel's desk to inquire about the piece of luggage that needed to be taken back to the States. The piece of luggage was gone. When they asked who had taken it, the captain told Stephan that Raymond had simply walked out with it!

Around 10:30 A.M. Tuesday morning, Raymond called the children and told them another one of his fairy tales—it turned out to be a horror story. Raymond explained that during the flight he heard the voice of God saying to him, "Why have you forsaken me?" So he told the children he could not come back; he had to stay in Kuala Lumpur. After Melanie begged him to come back, so that he could explain his sudden decision, he promised he would be there in a few hours. But he never showed up. We never saw him again.

The children—especially Melanie—were devastated. This supposed man of God had lied and cheated all the way through. When he left the hotel, he also left the children with an hotel bill amounting to over $1,500, knowing they had no money. He lied to Melanie, he lied to Stephan, he lied to my wife, he lied to me; but worst of all, he used the name of God to cover his lies and actions.

Stephan and Melanie called a pastor in Singapore they had previously met and told him the story. Pastor Prince took the time to come to the hotel. He also, as the church pastor, paid the hotel bill and gave them pocket money.

Only upon their return to the Los Angeles airport would they find out the real story. They called Don Mandell, and Melanie really poured her heart to him. From Mandell she learned with consternation that Raymond had never left his wife like he had us believe!

Raymond lied about his marital situation, he lied when he said he wanted to divorce, he lied because he claimed to be a man of God. The Scriptures are very clear on this subject: all liars shall perish.

The children arrived in Orlando March 18, at 2:00 in the morning. They were broken-hearted, devastated; they felt abused, cheated, and rejected. If you think this is the end of our torments with Raymond and his peers, wait till you read the next chapter. You will be astonished at the way "beautiful" Christian ministries mistreated a simple and naive family. You will discover the true faces of Morris Cerullo, John Avanzini, and Roberts Liardon.

CHAPTER TEN
A VALLEY OF TEARS

The children came back home early Thursday morning on March 18, after four straight flights from Singapore. They were exhausted and worn out; but mainly devastated. No words could describe how we felt about what Raymond did to Melanie and Stephan. What seemed to be the end of a nightmare simply turned into its continuation.

We felt helpless in comforting our daughter. She was broken and she could not believe that someone had so abused her feelings. It took her months to recover from those lies, but she came out of it stronger then ever.

How simple and naive to believe in their imaginary themes. We were simply too innocent and trustful. But how could we have known better?

We all attempted to get some rest before dawn. In the morning we called some of the ministries who employed Raymond Mooi. As sure as the moon shines out of darkness, our revelation of the truth was going to expose their wickedness. We decided to contact only three of them. We wanted to be honest and transparent regarding this devastating adventure. The leaders of these three ministries are Morris Cerullo, John Avanzini, and Roberts Liardon.

We addressed our first call to Morris Cerullo. Of course, when you call these guys they are not available to talk to you. Even after I mentioned the name of Raymond Mooi to the secretary, she refused to transfer the call to Morris. Instead, she transferred me immediately to the Director of Operations Don Mandell. He serves as a liaison between Morris and the rest of the world.

I related the complete story to Mandell. We wanted to meet and explain the facts to Morris Cerullo in person. Mandell knew the story. Melanie had told it to him at the Los Angeles airport.

That day Mandell disclosed the facts that Raymond had never left his wife. He confessed that Raymond and his wife had even spent the previous Christmas with the Mandells. At this point Melanie felt even more shocked. She could not believe that during all this time her fiancé had never left his wife.

Mandell seemed very sympathetic to our concerns. He said that he would talk to Brother Cerullo, and he would call back as soon as he gathered more details.

The following morning, March 19, at 8:30 A.M., Don Mandell called back. He said that we could not meet Mr. Cerullo. Again I insisted, but Mandell denied my request. He also added that the ministry was putting Raymond and his wife under a six-month surveillance. This included a period of marriage counselling and, to prove his repentance towards us, Raymond was wiring $1,500 to my attention in Orlando. Well, that sum amounted only to the value of the clothes and the bracelet he had stolen from the children.

It was not a repentance, because one can only repent if he has a true and honest heart. He only remitted the value of stolen goods. However, no amount of money would stop us from putting Raymond Mooi out of circulation. There was and still is no bribe to keep us quiet.

Nevertheless, Don Mandell added that he would try again to convince Cerullo to see us. We had waited so long to get our promised appointment with Benny Hinn, that we were in no mood to wait for Mr. Cerullo. A few days passed without an answer from them. So I called back. This time the attitude of Mandell had totally changed. Surely, he and Cerullo had figured that $1,500 would buy our silence. They were wrong.

The next minister I contacted was John Avanzini. The great majority of the phone calls originated from our home and were paid for by us. Those people are not willing to spend a penny unless they know they can get it back.

So I called John Avanzini—Brother John, as he likes to be called. His secretary answered the phone. I told her a part of the story, and then she interrupted me, "Mr. Avanzini is about to leave for the airport. But he will take time to talk to you."

As I related the story to Brother John, I felt no compassion whatsoever from him. I could sense that he was more interested in measuring the bad effects that situation could have on the financial aspect of his ministry. He said that he would check the matter.

I also asked him about the books Raymond had given me to translate. Well, to my great surprise, Brother John knew nothing of the situation. He said he never asked Raymond for any translation, but that he would verify this with some members of his staff and get back to me.

Our patience regarding the time we had to wait to receive a phone call had been reduced to its minimal limit. So after a few days, I called Avanzini's office.

Brother John was not back from his business trip, but they transferred me to his wife, Patricia. She felt sorry for what happened to our family, but she affirmed that their ministry had no intention to pay for books they had not ordered.

We had been duped by another of Raymond's lies. And he had been watching Stephan and I working to exhaustion to translate books that he knew had never been ordered! How malicious and cruel can a man be! This guy is a sure threat to the Christian world. But big ministries keep on protecting him because he represents for them a sure and growing investment.

Pursuing our initial decision, we called the third minister, Roberts Liardon. Roberts knew us, for we had met him in his hotel room in Orlando during the World Conference. While the children were in Asia, my wife and I had also volunteered as head ushers for Roberts in his three-day conference held at the Hyatt in Orlando. In those days, Roberts called us his French friends.

So we contacted Roberts. First Stephan talked to him; then Melanie pursued the conversation. Roberts showed compassion and said that Raymond acted dishonestly, and added that she had no reason to feel guilty. Finally, Stephan told him that we had to go to Montreal and both agreed that we would call him again upon our return from Canada (this trip is related in Chapter Twelve).

Therefore upon our return to Orlando on Wednesday, April 21, we called Roberts Liardon's ministry. Roberts was not available, so we left a message with his secretary. Days passed without an answer. We called again, and again, and again. We could not reach Roberts.

The following day we called Mandell because we still wanted to talk to Morris. For Mandell had told us, before our departure for Montreal, to keep in touch. Morris not only was refusing a meeting, he would not even talk to us. And the decision was final.

We were certainly not ready to take No for an answer. Our experiences had been too painful for us to remain passive.

Melanie wanted to talk to him. Mandell, who has children of his own, treated her like a nobody. He was very rude. So Nicole grabbed the phone and really unloaded on him. She told him that we would stand firm, and that we claimed the justice of God on Cerullo and on his ministry. Nicole also added that things would not stay as they were, and that we would pursue and make sure that Raymond Mooi was put out of circulation. The gravity of his actions demanded a demotion from his position until we received solid proofs of a sincere repentance and a true rehabilitation.

That was the last contact we had with Morris Cerullo's ministry.

Finally on Friday, April 30, Stephan tried once again to reach Roberts. But he was asked to talk to Don Steiner, one of Roberts's assistants—or may I say one of Roberts's duplicates.

Steiner could not accept the fact that we were revealing Raymond's wicked behavior to other ministries. For you see, he was an indispensable tool for their ministry in Asia. Seeing that those three "men of God" did not even bother to call us back, we had decided to call his other employers to warn them of Raymond's true nature.

Surely one of those ministers would listen and stand for righteousness. A married crusade director who commits himself into a wedding engagement in the United States is certainly not a common situation in the Christian world! I am not talking about low-level ministries here but about some of the biggest charismatic or evangelical ministries in the United States. These include people like Morris Cerullo, John Avanzini, Roberts Liardon, R.W. Schambach, Marilyn Hickey, Mike Evans, Carman, Carlton Pearson, and others. Raymond Mooi represents the reason of their success in Asia.

Steiner talked to Melanie, but after she mentioned that she hoped for some justice, he insulted her by saying that her heart was filled with hatred. This is strange behavior from a man who acted very nicely when he had previously met the children in California. These guys are really full of love!

Then Stephan talked to Steiner, and again Mr. Steiner was rude, but mainly frustrated because we had contacted other ministries. We had to do so because we wanted justice to be done. Roberts Liardon and his staff had changed their initial attitude towards us, and a question came in my mind: shall I call him in the future Roberts "Liar"don, or Roberts Liardon?

It is clear to see that Cerullo, Avanzini, and Liardon got together and decided to protect their man in Asia. Even thought they knew all the facts—true facts that have never been denied; even if they had put him through counselling, Raymond continued to work for these ministries. Pastor Prince revealed this truth to Stephan during the course of a phone conversation shortly after this revelation. Pastor Prince and Pastor Kong held the responsibility of counselling Raymond and his wife.

Even if they knew that their man was a liar, and a crook, and a thief that stole money from them, they preferred maintaining a business relationship with Raymond.

You can see that their heart is more inclined towards money and material profits than it is towards God's children. They should have never retained financial ties to a man of that nature.

That period had to be the toughest in our lives. We felt like truth did not exist anymore and questioned ourselves about the integrity of some Christian ministries. All the lies those guys tell you, it is unbelievable. They preach about love and Jesus, and their heart does not even contain one ounce of compassion and honesty. We do not love the same God. Their god is money, power, greed, corruption, and hypocrisy.

We were rejected by ministries we respected because we thought they were from God. Those adventures, however, showed us that those guys exploit God's name for their own benefits. No wonder they are very good friends with Benny. They flow in the same spirit—the greedy spirit.

Now let me brief you on John Avanzini and Roberts Liardon.

John Avanzini is well-known in the Christian circles as the "Prosperity Preacher." He distorts the Bible and makes people believe that if you give a certain sum of money to his ministry, or to the ministry he preaches for, God will give you back one hundredfold. This way he collects from innocent people fabulous sums of money for himself and for his peers. He flies first-class, lodges first-class, and eats first-class. He does not hide his luxurious lifestyle because he has to project the success of his enterprises.

John Avanzini is a regular guest when TBN presents its *Praise-a-Thons*. He has even written a book titled, *It's Not Working, Brother John*, in answer to those who question the validity of his teaching, or have not received their expected financial harvest. In his book, Brother John puts the blame on virtually everyone and everything: no tithing, no faith, not trusting God's man, etc.; except blaming himself and his false teaching.

Roberts Liardon is an enterprising preacher who has established his headquarters in California. He pretends in his book titled *I Saw Heaven* that he took an extensive tour of heaven at the age of eight, and that during that tour he had an encounter with Jesus Himself. Roberts relates that Jesus showed him a storage house filled on one side with arms, fingers, and legs; and on the other side were shelves filled with little packages of eyes: green ones, brown ones, blue ones, etc. The building contained all human body parts that people on earth need.[1]

Liardon also claims that, while visiting heaven, Jesus ordained him as a minister. Liardon supposedly saw Him a second time, but he refuses to talk about it. The third time he saw Jesus, he was eleven years old. Roberts says that Jesus walked through the door while he was watching the sitcom *Laverne and Shirley* on television. He writes:

> He came over and sat down beside me on the couch.... He looked at me and said, "Roberts, I want you to study the lives of my generals in my great army throughout time. Know them like the back of your hand. Know why they were a success. Know why they failed. And you'll want nothing in that area."
>
> He got up, walked back out through the door, the TV clicked back on, and I resumed watching *Laverne and Shirley*.[2]

It seems inconceivable that after having an encounter with Jesus Himself, he went back to his TV sitcom! I need to explain something here. Roberts was raised by his grandmother Gladoylene who has greatly influenced him. He loves her dearly and sometimes brings her with him in his crusades. Roberts has declared that as a young boy, he and his grandmother locked themselves up in a room for hours. Watching her pray, he said he knew his grandma so well that he would bring her a glass of water even before she asked.

Children of that age have fertile imaginations. Several hours spent behind a locked door watching a person pray would most probably perturb any child, and make him vulnerable to visions and hallucinations. For Roberts, his grandmother represents a spiritual example. Surely he has no intention of disappointing her.

Many of Liardon's preachings are given in conjunction with fake prophecies (him too!) He preaches, and suddenly he starts speaking in tongues—a phenomenon known as glossolalia. And then he interprets his own gibberish into English. I heard him at OCC "prophesy" things that everybody in the church knew!

Roberts is a close friend to Bill Byrd, the same man OCC fired as school principal. Roberts has started a network of churches in Florida. The two churches, located in Orlando and Ocala, are pastored by Bill Byrd and Richard Perinchief, respectively—two man ordained by Roberts Liardon. These two men were both on the pastoral staff of OCC, and surely Roberts has received some spicy information about Benny Hinn's church.

Cerullo, Avanzini, and Liardon should bear in mind that, "Judgment for an evil thing is many times delayed some day or two, some century or two, but it is sure as life, it is as sure as death."[3]

CHAPTER ELEVEN
"HINN"SIDE EDITION
BENNY "HINN"SIDE OUT

While the children were traveling throughout Asia, Nicole and I, like millions of other viewers, watched the televised national exposé of Benny Hinn and his "healing" ministry on *Inside Edition*. In this exposé, Benny's exhibition, while interviewed by the journalist Steve Wilson, can be valued as an Oscar winning performance.

Shortly after that broadcast, Christopher Hinn was politely asked to resign—because of the pressure—from the board of directors of the church. It is also at this time, that they returned my translation in an envelope that included a letter typed on Benny Hinn Media Ministries stationery dated February 28, 1993—a Sunday! I will never know who to thank because no one dared to put his name at the bottom of the letter. Very strange!

Even if the journalists who investigated Benny and his ministry in March 1993 did a magnificent job, the truth of the matter is that even after this national disclosure, Benny and his crew kept sailing along a rather calm sea.

I traced back the program *Inside Edition*. In doing so, I discovered so many discrepancies that I felt obliged to dedicate a chapter on the subject.

The three dominant details covered by the investigators were the veracity of the healings, the promiscuous manner that Benny's miracle team dealt with the financial side of the crusades, and the expensive lifestyle of the "great man."

The facts I am citing in this chapter are taken from *Inside Edition*, from *Channel 6 NEWS (WCPX-TV)* in Orlando, and from the TBN program *Praise the Lord*. The counterparts and commentaries on the facts are genuine and my own.

Are the Healings for Real?

Benny proclaims proudly during crusades, "People, everybody here can be healed tonight."[1] That is a very bold and dangerous statement because of its impact on people. Nothing is impossible to God and if He wants it, everybody will be healed; however Benny fails to mention that it has to be according to the will of God, and not according to a statement given to an excited crowd ready to believe anything he says.

Words proclaimed with such authority though, place those dear people who are not healed in a precarious situation. They may even think that they lacked faith, or worse, that God did not care for them. The surprising conclusion, however, that one will face regarding the evidence of healings or miracles claimed by contemporary self-proclaimed faith healers is this: Despite their claims, there exists no irrefutable proof.

Where are the cases of organic diseases completely cured? Their absence is striking. Where are the cases which are physically obvious to anyone—with or without medical knowledge—and for which you can have immediate evidence that their appearance has really changed? Instead, what is mostly presented by those "anointed" ministers are cases that have been manipulated and do not stand up under scrutiny.

The case of Jane Watts is an example of "healing" that does not stand. She says, "I was watching Pastor Benny on the TV and Pastor Benny said that God told him that there was somebody that is having problems with their left side, and I was healed that easily."[2] Anyone can see that she is still limping, her paralysis still shows on her whole left side. Even the TV reporter Mary Hamill noticed and commented on it.

One has only to observe individuals leaving the service and returning home as ill as when they arrived. Leaving a "Miracle Service" some are confused, others in tears, or worse devastated and hopeless. It is a heartbreaking moment. When the emotional highs are over and reality hits again, individuals may actually be in a worse state than when they came in. Who is to blame? Certainly not the victims. They are only prey in the hands of ravenous wolves.

In Benny's "healing" services people are often very desperate, and the slightest deception can cause them great harm. He often mentions that he has given his life to help people. The help he pretends to give them, however, is nothing but another sure way he uses to suck more money from them.

Several "miraculous healings" that took place in the crusades displayed on *Inside Edition,* and then later shown on his television program were not genuine. After a thorough examination of those healings, it was proven that they had been orchestrated by Benny's miracle team and were played on television to financially benefit them.

The first case involves a lady who suffered from a brain cancer. Her family had driven her hundreds of miles to attend the crusade and hoped the cancer would be cured that night. When she got on stage, Benny under the "anointing" touched her saying, "Every bit of it goes."[3] The lady fell on the platform. Three weeks later, the confident lady felt sure the X-rays would show no cancer. While Benny used her healing on his daily television program, she went to her doctor for further tests. Unfortunately, she was not healed.[4] What a tragic story.

The second case refers to Candy Brusseau. She is even cited in Benny Hinn's book *Lord, I Need a Miracle.* The book states, "Candy Brusseau was born profoundly deaf in both ears."[5] Her doctor, Howard House, who has treated her for more than thirty five years, declares, "She was born with a severe hearing loss, she was not born profoundly deaf."[6] So why did Benny claim on the platform that she was healed of a natal profound deafness? Again they manipulated a fake healing case to promote their ministry.

The same phenomena happen in his church. Mary Hamill of *Channel 6 News* reported the following statement made by Mr. Bob Eldredge—a long-time member of OCC:

> Benny Hinn called out someone in the balcony and said that God was healing a tumor in the neck, and at that instant my wife felt a warmth sensation and the tumor disappeared. The cancer went into remission, but eventually it came back and she died.[7]

What a sad story.

Once again the hopes of innocent people had been raised only to be destroyed by a temporary healing which resulted in the death of the person. It has been reported that mesmeric treatments have produced instantaneous relief from ailments which had been deemed incurable. But in many cases the symptoms reappeared a few days later.[8] Nevertheless, after the loss of his wife, Mr. Eldredge and his three children kept attending OCC and believing in the anoint"Hinn"g.

The icing on the cake in the investigation is the actress, hired by *Inside Edition*, who made Benny Hinn believe that she had received a complete healing from polio. *Inside Edition* asked her to see if Benny's miracle team could tell if her story was not true, to see if it would matter, to see if he would ever check. No one checked her out, but the episode was shown on his TV program *This is Your Day*. He knew the sequence could surely help squeeze bigger donations from his followers.

The following Thursday night on the TBN broadcast of *Praise the Lord*, he tried to get out of that scheme by saying the lady was the best actress he had ever seen. In an attempt to take some blame and pressure off of him, he went on and on about the girl's performance. Here are his exaggerated congratulations:

> The girl that came on the platform was the best actress I had ever seen. I, honestly to tell you. I have never seen someone act as good. She was fabulous! I would like to call her and tell her how impressed I was. I'm serious, she was incredible! That lady could make it very big in the movies. She is incredible.[9]

An actress that was so good she could fool a man who pretends to have a big "anointing" on his life! If Benny performed, as he claimed, under the anointing, and if his anointing is from God, how could he be fooled? Can we take for granted that this lady had more acting talent than some of Benny's friends; professionals like Dyan Cannon and others?

When asked by Tony Pipitone if he was afraid that people are going to think he is a fraud, Benny answered, "I know I'm not a fraud, what matters is what I know."[10]

Wrong Benny! What really matters is what people know. As you can realize, folks, the opinion that you people might have—even the ones who generously send money to his ministry—about Benny and his ministry really doesn't matter to him. He cares only for himself. So people, how much do you evaluate the opinion the "great man" has of you money purveyors?

Financial "Hinn"tegrity

The second aspect in the *Inside Edition* investigation that caught my attention was the way Benny's crusade team handled the envelopes containing the offerings. Benny tried to cover up that awful mishandling, the unheard fact that those envelopes—having prayer requests written on one side—had been emptied of their monetary contents and then simply left on the floor.

He said that two volunteers were responsible for dropping the envelopes on the floor. Well, I cannot believe Benny's version, nor can I believe that a big ministry like his would leave envelopes containing money with some volunteer workers in a room, without any supervision from an accountable staff member. Has anybody from his ministry showed these people how to handle the envelopes? Or is it that the volunteers acted as they were told to?

Benny made a very strong statement concerning that incident. Here is what he said to Tony Pipitone of *Channel 6 NEWS*, "It happened in one crusade. It's not my policy, it's not our policy, and whoever is responsible for that will be fired. It's just that simple."[11]

He repeated the statement the following Thursday on *Praise the Lord*:

> The staff members that I know...like Kent Mattox, David Palmquist, and others that work with me closely would never purposely leave prayer requests behind them. Never. We don't know how it happened but I'll tell you this as I said on *Inside Edition*: whoever is responsible for this will be fired."
>
> Paul [Crouch] I will not allow a man to betray trust like that...and for a man who works with me or for me, or for a volunteer betray that trust; he does not belong in the ministry in any way, shape, or form. Because God's people are important.[12]

Well if Benny is a man of honor and integrity, like he pretends to be, he will have to fire his administrator Gene Polino who stepped on those prayer envelopes, as everybody saw on the *Inside Edition* videotape. His dear administrator walks all over those envelopes without even bothering to pick them up. He was in too much of a hurry, and was too busy securing his big briefcase.

The argument Paul Crouch gave to cover up the "great man" does not stand. Paul's argument was:

> "If reporters would go to that length to try to discredit someone like yourself [Benny], how do we know they didn't have representatives, volunteers in the counting room, where the mail was opened."[13]

Polino does not work for *Inside Edition* but for Benny's ministry; yet he did not even bother to pick up the prayer requests he saw on the floor. Paul Crouch would really say anything to cover up someone like Benny Hinn who is credited for bringing, when he appears on TBN, the biggest donations.

Interestingly a similar incident occurred some time later in Basel, Switzerland. After a healing service in which Benny's organization collected three hundred thousand Swiss-Francs (approximately $250,000), empty money envelopes with prayer requests on the rear were simply thrown away.[14]

On *Inside Edition* and on *Praise the Lord* Benny proudly declared that a man that betrays trust "does not belong in the ministry." This time who's the betrayer, Benny?

Benny Hinn's Lifestyle

The third facet of *Inside Edition* features Benny Hinn's extravagant lifestyle. Many statements made by Benny on *Inside Edition,* and a few days later on *Praise the Lord* are quite contradictory.

He said on Channel 6 News, "I have never taken money from people on those crusades. I don't touch it. I don't touch the money that comes in through television, through the mail."[15]

How about the books, the audio and videocassettes that are sold in bookstores, in the crusades, via his TV program *This is Your Day* and his monthly magazine? Doesn't he consider these sums as money coming from the crusades, the TV healing ministry, or through the mail?

Benny declared to Paul and Jan Crouch that the royalties he got were from his books. "These [books] are my books," he said, "I work on them on my own, I work on them in my house...the church does not own the books."[16] How do we explain the fact that in the acknowledgements of his book *Good Morning, Holy Spirit* he thanks Nancy Pritchard, Sheryl Palmquist, and Gene Polino? Most probably, these staff members helped in various aspects of the book during the church business hours.

He also declared to Paul and Jan, talking about his expensive house, "The house is my home, I pay for it from my salary. My church does not pay for my home."[17] Is it not surprising that he later declared to Charisma magazine when asked about his lifestyle, "My salary is $116,000 plus a housing allowance."[18] Same question, but a very opposite answer.

He further said to Paul and Jan that he was selling his Mercedes-Benz car. Then he said to Bill O'Reilly that the car was sold, and that he was going to drive an American car. Benny said:

> Let the world know I am not attached to materialism...there is no need for me to drive such an expensive car...the image today that I must represent is that of an honest person who is sincere and really wants to do right in the sight of God and man.[19]

Talking about image, is it to sharpen his image that he wore his big diamond ring on *Praise the Lord,* but his regular black stone ring in the interview with Steve Wilson on *Inside Edition?* Is he trying to project two different images, one for the Christian world and one for the secular?

Then in the same interview Benny gave to *Charisma* in August 1993 he declared, "But I am replacing it [Mercedes Benz] with an American-made car, a Lincoln, because I don't want my lifestyle to cause anyone to stumble."[20]

In a broadcast on TBN he said, "Let me tell you what God showed me. Paul the apostle in First Corinthians, Chapter 8, states this: he said, `If eating meat offends my brother, I won't eat it'....Why should I drive a Benz and hurt a soul?"[21]

Well surely few people know that Benny, aside from driving his Lincoln automobile, also drives a British-made vehicle. He got himself a top notch white Range Rover vehicle—the most expensive of its category.

Benny has often declared that the Bible does not say that ministers have to be poor, and that if you serve the Lord, He will meet your need not your greed. The fact that he and his wife (two adults) drive three vehicles, is that considered a need or a greed? Is he not afraid his new image might hurt a soul?

Three times he states that one who betrays his trust, thus hurting his ministry and the kingdom of God, will be fired. When Kent Mattox did not call me after Benny told me he would, therefore betraying his trust, why wasn't he fired?

It took *Inside Edition* many efforts to get to Benny. He granted the fact on *Praise the Lord* as he explained the situation, "When I found out that *Inside Edition* had called, and I only knew of one phone call that they had made, and of course later I discovered there were many letters and things like this...."[22]

All the letters and phone calls that come in for Benny Hinn are channeled to his personal secretary, Nancy Pritchard. What happened to all these phone calls and letters addressed to him? Nancy has not done a first-class job, so she has hurt the ministry. She also has to be fired. So will he stick to his word, or is it another of his flamboyant statements that he made to impress the church and accentuate the fact that he is the boss?

I have to tell you a startling story that involves three members of Benny's staff. These three persons are better known as the infernal trio. His mother once had a dream in which God showed her three members of his staff who are not from God, but evil. Mrs. Hinn called her son Benny at three o'clock one morning and told him about her dream.

She revealed the identity of the three persons to him: they were the church administrator Gene Polino, his assistant Brian Lightfoot, and Benny's personal secretary Nancy Pritchard. We asked Mrs. Hinn if that story was true. The sweet lady did not say a word, but simply bowed her head as a sign of approval. This hallucinating story was confirmed to us by at least two persons involved in Benny's own Board of Directors.

Benny often said in the church that every time his mother gives him advice, he listens carefully. Well he certainly did not want to listen to this.

Here is one of the most amazing statements made by Benny on *Praise the Lord*:

> I never deceived anybody purposely or knowingly, never lied purposely or knowingly.... I fear God too much to tell you one thing and do another...it terrifies me at times to think what will the Lord say to me before millions or billions in heaven: Benny you said this, and you did that.[23]

Here we face another problem. Either Benny does not have a very good memory, or he is not conscious of the things he says, or he simply is a liar. He lied to us when he said in his office behind the stage and with many witnesses present, "I'm going to help you get your working permits, and I'm going to put you to work." So when Benny claims that he has never purposely or willingly deceived somebody or lied to somebody, what can we conclude? How will he answer the Lord's statement—Benny you said this, and you did that.

Has Benny Hinn really changed? I suggest to you, in the light of the information contained in this book, that he and his ministry have only changed on the surface. The facade has been modified to appear more righteous. It was only a shallow transformation.

When asked by Bill O'Reilly if it matters to him if some people feel he is a fraud, Benny answered, "All I know is the ones who know the Lord, the ones who are Spirit-filled know if I am or if I'm not. The Body of Christ knows who's real and who's not."[24]

Well, Benny was right on this one. The ones who are Holy Spirit-filled really do know.

Chapter Twelve
Oh! Henry

After our obnoxious experiences with Cerullo, Avanzini, and Liardon; as well as the fiendish way Benny Hinn and some of his staff members treated us, we felt pretty rejected and forsaken.

It occurred to us that it was the perfect time to leave for Montreal because we had a few things to settle. We lived by faith, and individuals would make donations to help us survive in our trials. This is how we could afford to go to Montreal. Perhaps the trip would help each member of the family to heal some wounds caused by this nightmare.

We set the departure date for Monday, March 22. It promised to be quite an experience for we would travel by Greyhound bus, a thirty-hour nonstop adventure!

The children had arrived less than a week earlier from Asia. So we hopped in the bus heading for Montreal. It turned to be quite an experience. Despite a few inconveniences, we finally arrived in Montreal and went to a friend's apartment where we would sojourn.

I mentioned earlier that Christopher Hinn had asked me if I wanted to help his brother Henry. Henry was planning a crusade in Montreal for the end of March. At that time I agreed, and made collect calls to Vancouver. I dealt mainly with George Kane, the man designated by Henry to work with me in setting up that crusade.

I supplied George with all the information I could gather; that is, names, addresses, and references of people I knew who could help Henry in Montreal. I also cautioned George about one ministry in Montreal with whom they should not get involved. That ministry had—and still has—a filthy but well-deserved reputation.

Unfortunately George Kane did not make it to Montreal. He had to stay home and go under emergency heart surgery.

Henry and his men had met some friends of ours and others to prepare for his crusade in Montreal. We later learned that Pastor Alberto Carbone of church "Vie et Réveil" bullied everyone else. Carbone is a man who demands absolute control and does not tolerate competition. He was the one I had warned George Kane against.

"Vie et Réveil" is a megachurch located in a ancient movie theatre in downtown Montreal. The church is run by Alberto Carbone and a very influential group of women including the pastor's wife—a group that I have named "The Feminine Mafia." This does not come as a surprise since Alberto takes great delight in the company of women.

Carbone is the only preacher that I know who, after starting his ministry and church with his wife June, divorced her and remarried Manon, his secretary—a woman seventeen years younger than him.

His ministry is listed at the "Info-Secte" office in Montreal. "Info-Secte" is a nonprofit organization who specializes in finding and listing any church, organization, or movement that is considered a cult. One can find astonishing information in that office.

Carbone attended A.A. Allen Biblical College in Miracle Valley, Arizona, and was ordained under Allen's ministry in the 1970s. To say that he has been influenced by this renowned tent evangelist is an understatement. He has made the following statement his personal motto:

> Son, let me tell you something. Do you know when you can tell a revival meeting is over? Do you know when God's saying to move on to the next town? When you can turn people on their head and shake them and no money falls out, then you know God's saying "Move on, son.[1]

Carbone is known to have a "healing" ministry. Like all faith healers the healings are very seldom medically proven, and can sometimes lead to death because of negligence.

Before I go into details concerning these two deadly cases, let me tell you how I was, for the first time, victimized by a mesmeric operator.

During the summer of 1991, the ministry organized tent revivals in various cities. In the month of July they held one in a suburb of Montreal. They invited as a guest preacher James Cromwell, an American faith healer who had been in the trade for many, many years. According to Carbone and his staff, Cromwell had a fantastic healing ministry.

That Thursday night, Cromwell made an altar call for those who wanted to be healed. He said he felt a particular anointing for the healing of the eyes. I wore glasses because I had very poor eyesight, especially on the right side. So I decided to go up front and have Cromwell pray over my eyes. Here is how it happened.

I stood up front and, while I waited for Cromwell, Carbone who was sitting on stage looked at me and said, "Tonight is your night!" Then Cromwell came to me and asked for my need.

I told him about my bad eyesight. He grabbed my head very firmly, covered my eyes, and spoke very strange words that sounded like, "Beeli, beeli, beeli." He took his hand off my eyes and asked me if I could see better.

I told him it was a bit better, so he repeated the same gestures and pronounced the same strange words, "Beeli, beeli, beeli." When he unveiled my eyes, I could see more clearly than I had never seen. I was healed. Goodbye eye glasses! The crowd jumped to their feet. My wife and children were crying and rejoicing.

Unfortunately, the euphoria was short-lived. That night my healing did not take place, and I realized it when I drove the car back home. I had been a victim of the situation, caused by the manipulation of a mesmerist.

For several months I tried to convince myself and my family that I was healed. This pretention led me into lying about my healing. Then I questioned myself, I wondered if I was lacking faith, if I had done anything to displease God. I lied because I was trying to ascertain a healing that proved to be only temporary.

Being the center of attraction, what could I say to people around me the next day.

In some circles, the immediate explanation would have been, "You have lost your healing." Or something like, "You did not have enough faith." All the time, however, it had been only a deception. I have now decided to be honest. Multitudes live similar tragedies.

Following this tragic experience, I decided to change my nutrition. I must declare that my eyesight has improved, not because of a Faith healing "Miracle Service," but because I now take mineral and vitamin supplements, namely beta carotene.

In fact no genuine miracles can be claimed from that crusade featuring James Cromwell, aside some psychosomatic diseases that were supposedly healed. I will cite two other examples of false healings that occurred under Carbone's ministry.

The first case involves a young man named Martin, a very active member in the church. In 1991, Martin was told by Carbone that he was completely healed of AIDS. He strongly believed this affirmation. His "healing" under the ministry of Alberto Carbone proved to be false. He later died from the same disease.

It scares me to ponder the significance and the impact of believing such a claim. Martin had told us that he had jumped the gun a few times. The way he lived his personal life after his claimed healing, and how many people could be affected by the disease are questions that remain unanswered until this day.

The second case is as dramatic. The victim was Nicole, also a very active member of the church. Carbone told her that her breast cancer was healed.

That lady, her husband, and the rest of the family were very close to Carbone. The family was struggling financially. At one point they had nothing to eat. Nicole told us that neither Alberto nor his church helped them. She under went surgery for a double mastectomy, but died of cancer in 1994.

Obviously the healing claims of the ministry just cannot stand up to scrutiny. The fruits it bears reveal its true nature: That ministry was, and still is, not from God. May I say that Carbone's greatest miracles occur in the same manner as A.A. Allen's, that is, when he separates bills from billfolds. And about finances, people who had been attending that church for about ten years told me that they never heard, or witnessed an annual business meeting.

Alberto Carbone is malicious and money-minded. No respectable church wants to get involved with him because his ministry is rightly considered a cult. Despite his reputation, Henry Hinn decided to work hand in hand with him. Remember money talks.

Well I know for a sure fact that Carbone helped and is still helping Henry—only because Carbone wants to get to Benny via Henry. Carbone dreams to have a base in Florida.

Henry's crusade, scheduled for March 25 and 26, 1993, was held not too far from where we stayed. Therefore, we decided to go. As we expected, Carbone's army controlled everything. The greeters, the ushers, the offering collectors, the singers; a large percentage of the attendance emanated from his church.

I did not know Henry Hinn too well at the time. Yet when his brother Christopher asked me to give him a hand, I agreed because I believed in his honesty. You know, though, that blood is thicker than water; and the same blood that flows in Benny Hinn's veins, flows in his brother's.

When Henry arrived at the Montreal airport, a friend of ours picked him up in his limousine and drove him to the Four Seasons Hotel. Employees of the hotel can remember only one thing from Henry's visit; they remember that Henry took a safe off the car and secured it. Yes, his safe!

The first night, on Thursday, March 25, about twelve hundred people attended the meeting. That night Henry gave us some demonstrations of fake healing. If you think that Benny imitates Kathryn, I do not know how to describe the way Henry operates. He is nothing but a replica of his brother Benny—except that Benny has more class, which does not make him more honest.

That same night at the crusade we met Hank, a fellow that Raymond Mooi had introduced us to at Morris Cerullo's World Conference in Orlando. Hank is very similar to Raymond. During the conference, Hank had introduced us to his fiancé Nathalie. He did not say, however, that he already had a wife!

Henry utilized Hank as one of his right-hand men. In fact, he exploited him as a gofer, a sort of jack-of-all-trades. Hank is also an architect who was supposed to build the new church for Henry; but he later ran away to Indonesia with the construction funds! A very sure source had told me that Hank ran away with $500,000; and George Kane of Henry's ministry confirmed the facts, but added that the amount differed slightly.

How can a ministry allow an architect (one of its right-hand men) to handle such a sum of money this way? Somebody, somewhere, really missed the boat.

In the meeting scheduled for Friday, March 26, Henry used (or I should say tried to use) the same mesmerism power his brother Benny utilizes. Henry made a third-class show out of a service attended by honest people. In the same manner as his brother Benny, he started laying hands on people.

As time went by, Henry became more spectacular. He took a glass of water and splashed a man. This man fell like he had been hit by a brick. Henry went on and, using a pitcher of water, played around and made a spectacle with innocent people whom did not dare to resist him in front of such a big audience.

During this time he claimed that he was doing the work of God. He practiced the "anointing" like his role model Benny, and people walked right into it. People who attended the crusade had very mixed reviews concerning Henry Hinn and his ministry. Aside from Carbone's crowd, I must admit that the rest of the people who witnessed Henry's performance were not moved at all.

After the service, Hank—the playboy—invited us to have breakfast with him Saturday morning at the Four Seasons Hotel. We knew what kind of a guy he was, but we felt we had to go. We met him in the coffee shop. Well Hank thought that he could give us a little exhortation. He even brought his Bible to the table.

Always be very careful with men whom, regardless of their own private life, try to exhort you while they utilize the Word of God as a proof of their own spirituality.

Unexpectedly Henry walked in. He was about to sit by himself at another table, but we asked him to join us. He gladly accepted. We talked about his brother Benny and his ministry and about the lousy way they had treated us. With every phrase we said Henry agreed and added a spicy comment of his own. It looked like Henry did not care too much for Benny's staff, especially for Gene Polino.

Henry told us that his teachings and preachings on the subject of the Holy Spirit and the anointing had been copied by his brother Benny. According to him, Benny offers no original material—he has simply copied Henry's revelation. So is it Henry that imitates Benny, or Benny that imitates Henry? I don't know.

Before we left the coffee shop, Henry asked me if I wanted to translate his audiotapes into booklets. So he said, "I will see you tonight after the service. Don't worry, I'm not like my brother Benny. I will keep my word." He also invited us to Carbone's church, for he was preaching there that night. He insisted and said to Hank, "Reserve first-row seats in tonight's service for my friends here."

After the service ended, we tried to get in touch with Henry as he escaped by the back door. He had said himself that he would see us personally. Well Mr. Hinn made himself unavailable. We drove to his hotel and sat there in the lobby waiting for him. While we were waiting for Henry, Carbone arrived. He was very surprised to see us there.

Is it not strange that close to midnight, a pastor will visit the same pastor he had in his church twenty minutes earlier? Perhaps Carbone wanted to have a close look at Henry's safe!

Henry, like his brother Benny, is a man without integrity. He did not dare to show up. Instead he sent his gofer Hank to tell us that he could not see us. Hank was very rude to us in the lobby. It was very clear that Henry did not want to see us.

How can a man change his attitude towards people just like that? Either he lies when he promises you something, or he does not know what he is saying. Such an attitude is very disturbing. Either he listens to the call of money, or to the call of integrity. We left the hotel few minutes later, and headed for our friend's apartment.

When we got to our friend's place I had a message on the answering machine. Our upstairs neighbor in Orlando had called. He had bad news for us. Our nine-year-old cat had just died. He had also poisoned himself with fleas. We could not afford treatment. We had lost our second pet on account of fleas. Our dog Boule and the cat were part of the family, and losing them felt like losing a member of the family.

We also visited many close friends that we had not seen for several months. We had a great time, and in every home we were invited, people asked many questions about Benny Hinn and his ministry, for they had seen *Inside Edition* and were concerned. Of course we told them about the prophets, and about the promises Benny Hinn had made to us, as well as our hopes of having them fulfilled.

We had a good time in Montreal. However prophecies upon prophecies promised that we would see great openings upon our return. At the time we had yet to discover mesmerism and realize the yoke it demands. Such prophetic words as, "The Lord will take you back in areas where promises were made and the word of the Lord was not fulfilled," was keeping us chained.

Financially, however, things were difficult. Friends offered to rent us a car for a week. It came to us as the perfect solution. Once again the problem had been taken care of. A week would give us plenty of time to go back to Florida. We would even have a few days left on the rental to accomplish certain tasks. We were expecting great changes in the ministry of Benny Hinn, for he had said on television that the national exposé had opened his eyes. We were full of hope, and our hearts were full of joy.

So it was time for us to hit the road again. Our friend drove us to Plattsburg, New

York, where he rented the car for us. After goodbyes and farewells, we drove back to Orlando and to new adventures. We still had many things to settle, and too many questions remained unanswered.

CHAPTER THIRTEEN
HE GAVE THEM RICE AND MANGOS TO EAT

It felt nice to drive back to Orlando. I especially enjoyed the scenery in the Adirondacks. The state of New York really displays beautiful country sites. Then after you hit the turnpikes and finally reach Highway 95 and drive through Virginia, the Carolinas, and Georgia, you connect to Interstate 4 near Daytona which leads you directly to downtown Orlando.

As we anticipated, the weather was warm and very comfortable. The month of April is always nice in central Florida. So we arrived at the apartment, unloaded the car, unpacked the luggage, and took a look at our mailbox. We had the usual mail, except for a letter from Morris Cerullo's headquarters addressed to Mr. and Mrs. Stephan Brault!

The letter, signed by Don Mandell, thanked them for coming to the office. It was a nice attempt to cover up their irresponsible attitude during Stephan and Melanie's visit. It was like they ignored the fact that they were brother and sister!

Benny Hinn had declared on national television that he would correct things in his ministry. Perhaps, he had really repented. While watching the TV exposé and believing in his repentance, we were convinced that things would change. During the interview, Benny really acted as if he was the victim of some of his staff members. It seemed that they were responsible for hiding information from him. For us it confirmed what we already knew, and proved the validity of the rumor circulating in OCC concerning the infernal trio.

Under those circumstances, on Wednesday, April 21, we drove to OCC. To our surprise there had been no change. Gene Polino and Brian Lightfoot still held their controlling positions. The receptionist even informed us that Nancy Pritchard was presently working in her office. Resigned to the fact, we asked the receptionist to call her. Well, what do you know? Her phone line was busy. We waited, and waited in the lobby. Our call could not get through. So we left another message. Another one added to the extensive list.

The situation seemed hopeless. We decided to drive to Benny's secluded community and to refresh his memory about our appointment. What else could we do? It was about the only way left.

Thursday night, we jumped into the rented car and drove to Alaqua, the high-class and high-priced country club area where Mr. Benny and his family live. When you get to the very secluded club, the first thing you face is a booth guarded by a security guard, and protected by a security gate.

We drove to the booth and said to the security guard, "We have an appointment with Mr. Benny Hinn. Please tell him that the Brault family is here."

He took the phone and called Benny. He talked with him for quite a while, then hung up and he said, "Mr. Hinn says he does not want to see you."

We were that close to him, we had no intention of giving up so easily. So we questioned the guard, "Did you give Benny the correct name?" Then a State Trooper stood up in the booth and advised us very kindly to leave the premises immediately.

This shows you the bravery of Benny Hinn. He knew we attended his church, that we were not criminals; he knew we were not after his money, or after his wife or children. If we were so repulsive, why did the leadership use us in the Sunday school, prayer line, and choir ministry?

Benny's reaction left us breathless. By his attitude, he was now clearly establishing that he had no intention of meeting us. Why had he left us waiting all this time? It showed he didn't care, but he was not man enough to confront us.

Our prophecies, however, had drawn a different picture. It was consternation.

This was the turning point.

I then realized that I could not get Benny to fulfill his promises. I had tried through Nancy Pritchard; I had tried through Kent Mattox; I had tried through his brother Christopher. Benny did not want to respect his word, period. We never thought that people using the name of God had so little honor.

We finally understood that Benny enjoys being surrounded by dishonest people who are used to protect his image as an irreproachable saint. He employed that trick when he answered the accusations of *Inside Edition*. Benny kept on skirting his responsibilities, claiming he did not know about this and that. He turned the table to his secretary, his employees, and even to innocent volunteers.

Even the reporter Steve Wilson was misled. He commented on Benny, "I've got to tell you. I found him extremely sincere and somebody who wants to do the right thing. I get the feeling that perhaps there are people inside his ministry...." This is the impression Benny loves to project. The situation pleases and enables him to make some gains.

A member of Benny's Board of Directors once expressed, in my presence, his opinion on the environment around Benny, "There are some bad people around him, but hopefully one day it will change." And the wife of another director told us in a supermarket, referring to the same subject, "We don't understand why they keep the bad ones, and fire the good ones." That tells a lot.

Some persons make money to preach the gospel; but guys like Mr. Hinn, Mr. Cerullo, Mr. Avanzini, and Mr. Liardon preach the gospel to make money. The only language these guys understand is money and its benefits. Their heart has been replaced by a security vault. The key word that opens it: money. But they had better beware because money brings influence, influence brings power, and history has proven that power corrupts.

June 1 was nearing which meant we had to get out of the apartment. We had nowhere to go. There was absolutely no way we could move our furniture back to Canada. We had no money to rent a moving truck, no place to put our furniture, no place to sleep. The situation seemed hopeless, but we knew we had to hang in there.

This is the reason why we kept attending OCC. We had endured so many ordeals that it could not end in a cul-de-sac. Too many questions remained unanswered; too many things did not add up. We needed to understand. We had lost everything, we needed to gain the truth back.

Since the beginning, it had seemed odd that a minister of the Bible could be so rude and arrogant with his followers. Till that day we had excused him under the cover of his "anointing." There was then no doubt in our mind: such a fake cannot be used by God. We were still attending OCC to find out about the tricks of the "great man."

A prayer meeting was to take place the Saturday preceding our move. And Sammy Hinn would conduct it. This man truly loves God. His only handicap rests in the fact that he is Benny's brother.

Everyone in the church loved Sammy because he has a real burden for people. He was responsible for the ministry for couples, as well as the benevolent ministry. The latter is designed to help people in financial difficulties. In both positions he did a tremendous job.

We personally knew Sammy and felt the urge to talk to him. At the end of the prayer meeting we approached him and explained our desperate situation, stressing the fact that we had never been paid for the translation requested by Benny. After all, the laborer is worthy of his wages. He listened, showed compassion and said, "I can't do nothing but cover the cost of putting your furniture in storage. All I need from you is an estimate." Even as a brother he could not influence Benny!

He also insisted that we should come to church the following day. We accepted. This would allow him to give us the checks to cover the moving expenses.

Sunday morning, May 30, we headed for the church. As usual Benny arrived after thirty-five to forty minutes of songs and worship—he always comes up on stage at this point and then takes full control of the service. I never could understand why he cannot arrive on the platform before a service begins.

Now I can.

Benny intentionally delays his arrival to allow the crowd's expectation to be built up. By that time, people have been singing, worshipping, and have reached a high emotional level. Thus when he arrives on stage, people wrongly see him as a deity, for they attribute the awe to his appearance on stage.

Once again Benny acts just like Mesmer. For Mesmer would be ready to start his séance only, and only when he felt he had the right conditions.

So that day, after leading the congregation in a few hymns, Benny started preaching. He put on quite a show. With tears in his eyes, he said that God had talked to him—which for Benny is not unusual!

The Lord had supposedly ordered him to minister to the poor, to feed the hungry, and to clothe the naked; not only the ones of his church, but all the poor of the world. And Benny added that if he would not listen to the warning, his ministry would be forgotten in three years. In brief, Benny confessed that he had changed.

That was a very bold statement because it placed him in a situation where he had no ifs, ands, or buts. God had spoken to Benny, and therefore he had no choice but to obey what God had told him, that is, help and feed the people.

Benny had therefore decided that the church would open a house dedicated to help the poor and needy. In order to fulfill the mandate, the church needed money; hence, they took a special offering that would serve only Compassion House, the new ministry of the church.

Congregations are always deeply touched when offerings are asked for the poor. Benny made sure that everybody understood the message clearly. He mentioned that the church already owned a house on the property that could be put into service for this purpose. But some repairs were required, and building materials would have to be bought. The manpower, however, would be provided by the church volunteers. He appointed a pastor and told his flock, "I will make sure that Pastor Mike does a first-class job."

The clearer the message, the bigger the offering. They raised quite a big amount of money, surely enough to buy new building materials and decent nonperishable food items.

There are a few things I would like to point out about the way Compassion House operated. In one occasion I had, just a few weeks after its opening, to go get some food. The lady greeted me was rude, an attitude that made me feel uncomfortable.

They helped us but the given quantity was not sufficient for a family of four. They gave us cans of soup, beans, two small boxes of rice, two boxes of cereals, and a bottle of shampoo. The items were all damaged, therefore all secondhand. None of those articles sufficed to cook a complete meal for four adults, but we could go to church with clean hair! There was no meat, no fruits or vegetables, no food vouchers. There must have been over fifty of those boxes in Compassion House, each filled with more or less the same items.

The behavior of the personnel and the type of food boxes they give do not meet the first-class treatment that Benny brags about so often. There is no reason that can validate that kind of attitude. The poor people should be treated the same way as the ones that live in a higher financial realm.

The second thing I want to mention relates to a friend of ours, a member of OCC, who had given quite a fair sum of money when they took the special offering for Compassion House. One day our friend decided to pay them a visit. He did not go to ask any for kind of help (fortunately he didn't need any) but he asked some questions about the ministry, and also wanted to visit the premises. Well, they refused him the right to visit the house he had financially helped install with his offering! Our friend did not appreciate the rudeness with which they treated him. Quite shocking, is it not! On what grounds can they refuse a member of the church making such a normal request? Perhaps they had something to hide.

The Compassion House is a good idea, even though it is only a cover-up. For not everyone knows that Sammy Hinn had put together in the month of December 1992, some fifteen months earlier, a very sophisticated project in OCC. With the help of the members of the church, some clothing firms, and with the support of doctors and nurses, Sammy put together a project to help the needy of the church and of the community.

During that weekend they helped over 200 families. They provided dental and medical help to all of them, they clothed all the children with three new outfits, and gave them toys, and stuffed animals. The parents were also given clothes. On top of that they had manicures and pedicures done to help them feel better. They received everything that enabled them to spend a wonderful Christmas season. What a beautiful demonstration of love and care. Those families really felt special.

The results were so encouraging and the project was so well organized that Sammy planned to do it again in the month of June, 1993. This time it would include a series of meetings between employers and inactive employees of the church who desired to work. Eventually, as he said, this would take place every three months. Sammy's project was first-class operation.

It never happened again and they have never mentioned it since. Later, Sammy Hinn was "prophesied" by Bernard Jordan, one of Bill Hamon's disciples and a close friend of the Lechners, that he would become an evangelist! The church leadership hypocritically pushed him out of his previous position. And as a last resort, he accepted his new assignment. Again a mesmeric prophecy was used to justify man's will.

The truth is that three weeks before Benny had announced to the congregation that Sammy would minister as an evangelist, we knew—behind the scenes—that his office had been emptied of all his personal belongings.

And surprisingly they come up, about fifteen months later, with the Compassion House. What a demonstration of kindness! Particularly after a national exposé on television. Even though Sammy's project was superior to Compassion House, Benny and his clique put an end to it.

I am positive that a lot of members have questioned themselves about the whole matter; but who will dare to challenge the church authority? A great percentage of the people attending OCC have left within six months of their arrival. There is such an enormous turnover in that church that you feel that you are an elder after you have attended for only a few months. The leadership knows the situation and takes advantage of it. They purposely keep a lot of information hidden from the public.

Well that Sunday morning, Benny had done it again. While he was preaching, many people in the church were sobbing. His words had deeply touched his congregation, and if you did not know the man, you could easily be fooled and believe in his story.

Sure there is a part of truth to it. Compassion House helped many needy people but there is always that question in my mind: Why did they dismiss Sammy's project when it proved to be excellent?

We returned to the church that Sunday night. Even if we didn't know where we would stay the next day, none of us was worried. We knew God would find a way.

The service ended and Sammy took us to his office where we gave him the estimates he had requested. We had come up with the best possible prices. A one-day truck rental would cost $87.26, and for the storage unit we found the best deal in town—only $56.25 for the first month.

Monday morning arrived. We got the truck, loaded our belongings, drove to the storage, and placed the furniture in such a way that our luggage could be easily accessible. Many good samaritans kindly offered to let us move in with them. In return, we did our best helping them around the house.

Financially, however, times were very tough. We had no income, and the little food we had we needed to stretch from one meal to another. I remember that for a whole month we could not—the four of us—total the amount of one dollar. On another occasion, while taking a walk, we felt very thirsty, but we had only one penny left. While walking along the sidewalk and the parking lot, we found twenty-four cents. That allowed us to buy a twenty-five-cent soda at a K-Mart store.

A good friend of ours who worked in a plantation brought us 100 pounds of rice, and every weekend he would bring us bushels of mangos. And some organizations gave us food boxes on several occasions.

In June 1993, John Avanzini held a series of meetings in a church not too far from where we stayed. It was for us an awaited occasion to meet face to face the man who knew Raymond Mooi so well, because we had to clear up some matters with him. So on the first night we arrived early and sat in the second row.

Some of his men came to talk to us. We introduced ourselves. One of them even wrote down our name. We told them that Melanie and Stephan had been in Asia to set up crusades for John. They acted very kindly and said they would inform him about our presence. When John Avanzini walked into the sanctuary he could hardly hide his embarrassment.

He knew about the connection between Raymond Mooi and us. He had talked to me on the phone when he had refused to pay us for the book's translations. He knew all that and, believe me, he felt he was being put on the spot. His countenance betrayed his embarrassment.

When he walked on the platform he was as white as snow. It took him quite a while to get back on his feet and start his preaching. I have already related the errors in John Avanzini's "hundredfold" message. I will not dwell on that except to say that by twisting the Scriptures, Avanzini sucks money right out of innocent people's wallets. He tricks you into believing that if you invest into his ministry—or others he supports—God will give you back one hundredfold.

A pretty sound investment, is it not? Let us make a rapid calculation. If you give $100 to John Avanzini's ministry (or as he says to God's kingdom), you will get in return $10,000. This is how he distorts the Bible. John Avanzini has turned a portrait of the communion that exists within the family of God into a selfish money-making business.

Brother John finally got his act together and gave the audience an economical thesis on Jesus's wealth. Of course he asked for an offering, and for that offering be our best. As soon as the meeting ended, one of John Avanzini's men signaled to me that Brother John wanted to see us. We accepted and followed him in the back of the church. Brother John was waiting for us. He took us into a room, invited us to sit down, and started his little speech.

First he said that he felt sorry for what had happened to us. Then he revealed that Raymond had multiple personalities (this is probably the reason why he cheated on multiple ministries!) Then he added, "Raymond is under a three-month probation but with full salary. His wife quit her teaching job so that she can be closer to him. They are both under counselling." He ended by saying that he had no intention of paying for the book's translations.

We also asked him about the deal between Morris Cerullo and the Malaysian conglomerate, namely the fact that the new owners were losing $80,000 a month. John agreed that for the Malaysians it was a bad deal, because they were losing more than $80,000.

At no time during the private meeting did we feel some kind of brotherly love. He had no compassion whatsoever, no feelings. He treated our conversation as a business meeting. A great demonstration of pastoral care!

His wife Pat told the whole crowd in a morning session that three months after she met Brother John he still bore no fruits. Time and events have proven that decades after their first encounter "Brother" John has not changed an iota and he still doesn't bear fruits. Some people call him Dr. John Avanzini. Well, perhaps he is a veterinarian.

This private meeting proved to us one more time that all those famous fake preachers, those illustrious "men of God," are in it for one major reason: MONEY. They evaluate a soul by the thickness of his wallet or by the importance of his assets. The meeting also proved to us that Brother John does not believe in his own teaching. His teaching of hundredfold returns is only a scheme.

For he had a perfect occasion to plant a "seed" by helping people in need, but he refused. Those guys are wealthy not because God blesses them; those guys are wealthy because they exploit innocent and gullible people. The only ones that prosper are those few individuals who are close to them, and part of their clique.

But the Bible is clear, "But whoever has this world's goods, and sees his brother in need, and shuts up his heart from him, how does the love of God abide in him?" (1 John 3:17). Many incidents and strange things happened at OCC during the following months. Many will surprise, amaze and shock you.

CHAPTER FOURTEEN
HANGING TO A AIR MATTRESS ON A RAGING SEA

Benny Hinn's ministry decided to increase its office space. The miracle crusades and the television program were getting more and more recognition; and as a result, more letters were coming in, more books and more tapes were being sold, etc. Therefore employees associated with that aspect of the ministry needed more working space.

In response to this, the ministry decided to build on the premises a two-story building. The ground floor would hold the bookstore; and behind it, the mailing and shipping room. The second floor would accommodate offices for the publishing department and for the crusade staff which comprised men like David Palmquist, Kent Mattox, and their respective secretaries, not forgetting Charlie and his secretary.

By doing so they liberated the church lobby from its very small bookstore, as well as some offices overlooking the sanctuary mezzanine.

One Sunday morning Benny informed the congregation about two new projects the ministry had planned. The first one linked to the church lobby, and the second to the air conditioning system of the sanctuary. He explained that the lobby needed to be enlarged so people would not have to wait outside in the rain, or under a hot Florida sun. That represented a long-term project, because they wanted to double the capacity of the lobby.

The second project dealt with the air conditioning system and the sound system. We all knew that they faced a major problem with the air conditioning system. Every time we would come early into the sanctuary, people would be covered with blankets or would wear heavy coats, or woolen sweaters. It was freezing in there, and many times during the services Benny would send David Delgado to temporarily fix it.

Benny stated that the sound system was ten years old. He added it could blow on us anytime during a service. He said, "The sanctuary needs a `facelift.' You people certainly don't want the sound system to blow out while I'm speaking." What a salesman this guy is! What a crowd manipulator!

He said the costs were estimated at approximately $100,000. What do you think he had in mind? Yes, he asked the congregation for an offering. I just cannot understand how a ministry that profits millions of dollars a year from offerings, donations, tithes, and sales needs to ask its members to give a special offering of $100,000 for a "facelift."

Would it not be better to have the big brass travel economy, and stay in good but less expensive hotels, and to eat affordable, nutritious but less expensive meals? Why would those guys—whose expenses are paid one way or another by the ministry—live the very expensive first-class lifestyle? They should reduce their expenses. I am convinced that by doing so they could easily save tens of thousands of dollars a year. That way the members of the church would not feel like a squeezed orange.

A few weeks later Benny told us that the cost of the projects would be higher. They would need a little bit more, something like $150,000 to complete the project. They had just realized that some offices up the second floor had to be moved, justifying the increase. Well the congregation believed his story one more time and they came up with the amount Benny asked for.

I must say that months later, the air conditioning system was far from being fixed. We were still freezing in the sanctuary. It felt like a winter in Alaska. And I know a man who gave in that offering and whose patience had so exceeded its limit, that he wanted to ask Benny to reimburse the money he had given.

As I mentioned in the preceding chapter, Benny, in his great "compassion," had decided it was time to feed the poor; not only the ones of the church, but the poor of the world. So to solidify his next move, and to make it more palatable to the church, Benny invited James Robison to preach one Sunday.

Some of you may know him well. James Robison is an outspoken Baptist preacher who was once considered the successor of Billy Graham. His ministry now helps to feed the hungry people in Africa.

After the preaching they took an offering—naturally—to help the poor and needy people of the world. Another major offering in a period of few months! Wallets were really getting squeezed. They raised quite a fair amount of money. Benny declared that he would go himself to feed the poor. He would go with the television crew so that we could also witness the great impact our donations made on these poor people.

We saw one day in the church an incident that really broke our heart. An incident that really showed us the true face of the "great man." During one of his news segment sessions, he talked about different subjects, then he asked the Sunday children caretaker to give him Eleasha, his youngest daughter. Benny took his own little girl in his extended arms, showed her to the people, carried her like you would carry a dirty diaper, and gave her to Fred Spring. The precious little girl, she is so cute. Even Fred Spring could not disguise his surprise.

When you watch his TV program *This is Your Day* and see him on the platform holding children in his arms hugging them, and even waltzing with them, it really makes you wonder. Benny shows two different images. But his flock at OCC love Benny so much that they forgive him for every thing he says or does.

Let me go back to that service with James Robison. The whole offering they raised was supposed, as Benny said, to feed the poor. And Benny himself would go. Well the issue turned out to be different.

Benny later told us that he could not go, his schedule was too full, that he could not find enough time for it. Benny said that he would send his wife Suzanne accompanied by Carol Kornacky, a preacher—supposedly delivered years earlier from various demons under Benny's ministry. I wonder if she has really been freed, for there is a lot of aggressiveness and anger in the lady. Then Benny's version changed again. Suzanne would go but with another lady. He finally made up his mind.

The other noticeable difference in Benny's words is that out of the amount he collected from the church for one specific purpose, Benny gave $50,000 to Mrs. Buntain, a Christian missionary who feeds people in Calcutta, India; and he also decided to give $50,000 to Mother Teresa.

Now we all know that Mother Teresa is a well-acclaimed international celebrity. Mother Teresa is a Catholic nun who rescues the poor from the streets. She has also been accused of doing things in the past for the sole purpose of being close to the renowned people of the world. Here is an extract of Mother Teresa's way of life:

> She turned up in Haiti in 1980, as an honored guest of the Duvalier family, and accepted the Haitian version of the Legion d'Honneur; garnishing the award with some words of her own about the great love that existed between the Duvaliers and the poor.
>
> She appeared in Central America in the mid-80s, accepting the Medal of Freedom from Ronald Reagan and making approving noises about the regimes then in power in Guatemala and El Salvador....
>
> Then there were her business dealings. How did she come to hear of Charles Keating, chairman of the Lincoln Savings and Loan company, now in jail for the biggest fraud in American history?
>
> In return for half a million dollars and the use of a Keating private jet, Mother Teresa showered blessings on this gentleman and gave him a personalized crucifix which he used to enhance his, as they say, credibility.[1]

Christopher Hitchens ends his article by commenting:

> She acts as spiritual camouflage for dictators and wealthy potentates—hardly the essence of simplicity.

Talking about wealth, you wonder why Mother Teresa has almost $50 million in one checking account in New York City, just naming this one. We all recognize that Benny loves to say that he knows some great personalities of this world. Why is it that Benny did not even bother to check on her true reputation? Is Benny impressed by her image, or her public relations?

One day I met George Parson, the man responsible for the editing and publishing of all the books and tapes of the ministry. George used to work for Billy Graham before he and his wife were asked to join Benny Hinn's ministry. I met Mr. Parson in the OCC bookstore and asked him if they were planning, in a near or far future, to sell and distribute tapes and books of the ministry in French.

Mr. Parson was honest and open with me. He told me that for the time being, they had no intention of going into the French market. He also said that seventy percent of Benny Hinn's teaching literature and tapes were being taken off the market—because they needed to be reedited! Now that brings one very important question to my mind. Benny Hinn likes to say that he hears from God, and that his teachings are given to him directly by the Holy Spirit. Well, if that is true, how is it that they have to reedit seventy percent of his teachings?

A respectable woman of the church came to us one day with a very, very strange story that had happened in the single's ministry. I will try to be as precise as possible in relating the facts. A few single ladies who attended the single's meetings at OCC had mentioned that the Holy Spirit visited them at night, and that they had sexual experiences with Him! The delicate information had even been related to the pastor of the singles.

Here is my point. I find it fearful and worrying that in a church where people are encouraged and taught to have a close relationship and experiences with the Holy Spirit, that members influenced by that teaching would feel obligated to attain the pastor's spiritual standards. The greatest danger, however, lies in the fact that innocent individuals take for granted that the Holy Spirit is in their midst, when in fact it is another; thus, forcing themselves into spiritual experiences and opening doors to lusty contacts.

Vincent Buranelli writes on the trance of Mesmer:

> The patient might lose consciousness or not. If consciousness remained, one or all of the five senses might lapse. Convulsions or catalepsy might supervene. The experience could be painful or pleasant, and one type generated a passionate desire on the part of the subject for its continuance—namely, the erotic trance.[2]

For many years and in numerous occasions we were placed in situations that allowed us to hear the most unusual insights. We have been in contact with people that held key positions in various ministries, and were told many revelations.

Here is another example of one of these situations.

It happened during a Sunday night healing service at OCC. These services were held on the first Sunday of the month. Needless to say, such services bring in a large flow of visitors from various areas. Melanie and Stephan were asked by a prayer partner to write down on standardized forms the testimony of people claiming healings that particular evening.

A lady who suffered from cancer, and who had flown with her husband all the way from Texas and arrived Saturday night in Orlando, came to OCC especially for a healing. My son and some friends had met them in a service station. The couple, looking for OCC, were helped by the children.

That Sunday night, the lady felt a heat in her body during the healing service. This manifestation was a sign of her healing for her. A pastor took her on stage and the "great man" laid hands on her, telling her that the cancer had gone, and advising her to get checked by her doctor. He even made use of his "anointing" to make her fall under the power.

After her personal encounter with the "great man," they accompanied her to the back where, with her husband, she met for a second time with our son and daughter. They conversed and exchanged their phone numbers.

A few weeks later she called Melanie. She was devastated because her cancer had not been healed. Her condition was even worse than before. Melanie did her best to comfort her, but what can you say, what can you do?

In his book *Welcome, Holy Spirit* published in 1995, Benny Hinn claims that in 1976 he was invited in Catholic Hospital in Sault Sainte Marie, Ontario by the Reverend Mother to conduct a healing service in the chapel (231). Hinn adds that during the service, patients all over the chapel were being healed instantly (233-34).[3]

However Lois C. Krause, the director of community relations for the town General Hospital, denied all that Hinn claimed, adding that "no patients left that day" due to miraculous occurrences. Furthermore, Mother Superior Mary Francis also disputed Hinn's account. She added that she did not invite him, but reluctantly allowed his chapel service. The hospital then released a statement including this remark: "No such events have ever occurred at General Hospital.... Mr. Hinn's claims are outlandish and unwarranted."[4]

And I later heard Benny Hinn say, "Every sick body will be healed tonight," in a crusade in Oklahoma City. After the *Inside Edition* exposé he became more careful, but such exciting statements are too tempting for the "anointed" faith healer.

During that same crusade in Oklahoma, his ministry gave half of its declared Thursday night offering to the Salvation Army, handing in a check of $27,251. That is a very generous gesture. What irritates me, however, is what Benny said during his program. He asked the millions of viewers and listeners to send in more money for the victims in Oklahoma City who had suffered from the terrorist attack on a Federal building.

Not that it is wrong. On the contrary. But to fulfill that request, people were advised to send their checks to Benny Hinn, Box 90 Orlando—Benny's headquarters in Florida. Then his ministry would send the amount received to the Salvation Army in Oklahoma City.[5] People were told to write on the envelope "For Oklahoma City."

The need was urgent. So why in the world did Benny ask the people to send their donations to his ministry in Florida, and not directly to the Salvation Army in Oklahoma City? And why ask them to write "For Oklahoma City" on the envelope and not on the check and envelope?

In that period where we met the lady from Texas, we were going to OCC for the fellowship, but mostly to know more about the true face of this fake faith healer Benny Hinn. We were also awaiting the answer for the green card lottery. Even that answer had been delayed.

At a certain time Benny claimed that he saw angels in the church. He even related that during a full year angels appeared to him every single night. And of course it reflected on his preaching in the church. One day he stopped preaching and said, "There are angels right there down the stairs."

Benny would sometimes say that he saw a mist floating on certain sections of the church. Once he walked down the platform and asked some persons if they could also see it. And they did.

The same was true with a few percentage of the subjects who had been entranced by mesmerists. They could not only feel hot and cold currents in their bodies, but also "see" dazzling bright lights. It is therefore not surprising that Benny and some of his followers see mists and fluids that they confound with angels and manifestations of the Holy Spirit. Benny has even said that he felt a circle of energy around him. This is mesmerism once again.

In one of his trips, Benny, accompanied of course by Gene Polino, Kent Mattox, a few bodyguards, and their TV crew, visited the garden of the Evangelical Sisters of Mary in Germany—a visit paid for by the church members and the ministry partners, naturally. Benny was impressed by those nuns, but not impressed as much as Mr. Polino. Mr. Polino was so impressed that Benny invited him one Sunday morning to share his feelings about and how deeply he was touched when they visited that garden. Gene Polino said, "I never felt the presence of God as strong as in that place."

This was a strange reaction from a man who has been shadowing the "anointed" Benny for many years. What of all the so-called miracles, all the so-called healings that Gene witnessed through the years? Even when Benny prayed on Gene's wife, even when God spared his own life after Gene had a serious heart attack; all those events could not move the heart of Gene as much as that location had!

There is another thing that worries me concerning Gene Polino. As the administrator of Orlando Christian Center and of Benny Hinn Ministries, he decides in what bank or trust the church and the ministry will deposit their revenues. Well, Gene Polino also sat— perhaps he still does—on the Board of Directors of the Winter Park Bank. Orlando Christian Center and Benny Hinn Ministries bank accounts are at the Winter Park Bank— the same bank!

Would you say that this awkward situation could lead into a conflict of interest? Is Polino on the bank's board because of the church's accounts, or are the church's accounts in the bank because Polino sits on their board?

Very rarely can we hear Gene Polino talk in the church. He does it as the church administrator at the business meetings, but even there he keeps it short and sweet. At on one business meeting we attended, Benny said, "I hate business meetings. So let's do it in fifteen minutes." Polino and Benny did not look too happy because members of the church were asking questions—too many questions on the financial aspect of the ministry.

CHAPTER FIFTEEN
WE HAD FAITH, HOPE, BUT WE COULDN'T FIND CHARITY

Many strange incidents happened while we attended OCC; some of which have already been related, but let me now describe a few others that need to be publicized. One of them implicated Rodney Howard-Browne, the South African preacher I briefly commented on in Chapter Four. When Browne was invited to preach at OCC in the fall of 1992, we knew nothing about him or his ministry. So when Browne spoke that Sunday night in the church, nobody really expected what was about to take place.

Rodney Howard-Browne's ministry is dominated by a laughing spirit. When Browne preaches—and he does it very seriously—people start laughing. They laugh uncontrollably, they just cannot stop. Soon you realize that hundreds of people are seized by that laughing spirit. Some roll over on the floor, some fall off their pews, but the result is the same—they just cannot control themselves. It is as if a freakish spirit inhabits them.

As long as he preaches, they keep on laughing and falling. During the course of the service, Benny walked off the platform and came to sit in the first pew. He stayed there for a little while, then walked back on the platform, waved at his friend Claude Bower to join him, and sat there chatting with Claude.

After Browne felt he had entranced enough individuals, he made an altar call for anyone who wanted to receive a refreshing touch from the Lord. People ran up front. Browne touched them and most fell down. At one point he even prayed over some of Benny's pastors.

Then Sammy Hinn, Dave Palmquist, and even Kent Mattox were under the control of the laughing spirit. That did it! Benny could not take it anymore. He stood up and, followed by Claude, walked right out of the service and into his office. It was the first time that I witnessed such an irresponsible and impolite attitude from a senior pastor towards his congregation.

The following Sunday, Benny gave us a real exhortation about Browne and his laughing spirit. He said that Browne's ministry was not from God, and that those kind of manifestations would not be tolerated in his church anymore. Benny should know better than that. His "anointing," just like Browne's "laughing spirit," is nothing else but mesmerism. The only difference lies in the fact that the occultic practice is exercised in a distinct manner to get a different result. Perhaps, Benny overreacted because Browne had stolen the show from him!

Browne was later invited to Oral Roberts University (ORU) to preach. By the way, ORU awarded an honoris causa doctoratus to Benny. He now admires Browne for the latter is now part of the clique, and is as popular as Benny in the charismatic circles. They have also participated in the same conventions, like in Tulsa, Oklahoma, in the summer of 1995. What an integrity he has!

Members of the Career and College ministry were asked to go on a missionary trip to Ecuador, South America. A large number of them had planned a trip of three months and, they were all fired up and ready to evangelize the whole country. Things turned out to be quite different. After two weeks in the mission field, they were told that the church had not enough money to keep them there, so they were ordered back home. These young adults were quite disappointed, to say the least. I have to comprehend that the ministry has enough money to pay regularly for first-class trips to preferred persons, but that they lack funds when money is needed to support their missionaries.

And they say they are not in it for money!

We kept on going to OCC, and at the end of November 1993 a Christian brother bought us a used car. He also paid for the tag and the insurance. That gift allowed us to move around and gave us the means of seeking out a solution to our problems.

Without even noticing it, we walked into the year 1994 but we did not attend the New Year's Eve service. We had decided to stop attending OCC because we just could not stand the atmosphere anymore. We felt we had reached our goal and now the time had come to find a way out.

We had heard through the grapevine that Benny had hired two new pastors; one to replace the youth pastor, and a second employed specifically to take care of the people. Benny had suddenly realized that a lot of people had deserted his church. He had visited his friend David (formerly Paul Yonggi) Cho who told him that OCC had a major problem: that more people were getting out through the back door, than they were getting in by the front door.

When explaining to his flock the observation of David Cho, Benny's first personal comment was, "When people are getting out, the tithes are also getting out!!!" What a great declaration!

In order to solve the problem, a pastor would therefore be hired to listen to people and their grievances. If anyone in the past had been hurt by the ministry, they needed to see that man. This was the first good news we heard from OCC for quite a while.

Therefore we drove to the church and walked directly to the reception desk. I told the lady that I needed to talk with the new pastor. She called him on the phone but he was busy. I got to talk to his secretary, gave her my name, and explained to her my situation. We wanted to collect the money they owed us for the translation we had done as per Benny Hinn's own request.

I added, "Tell the pastor that I must urgently talk to him." She did not seem to realize the seriousness of our situation. She took note of my name and request, and told me that the new pastor, however, would be busy for the next three weeks. Then he would have meetings with all the staff members. I thought they had hired the man to solve the people's problems, not to act as a human resource manager. She asked me to call back the next day, then she hung up.

I did not call the next day. Instead, I went directly to the church, for I knew too much about their voice mail policy. Again I addressed the receptionist telling her that I wanted to talk with the new pastor. As soon as I had given her my name, for she knew who I was and was following the orders she had received, she took the phone and called the security guards of the church. They considered me as a threat. The security guard who showed up knew me for quite a while, so he greeted me with a joyful, "How are you brother?"

What an uncharitable behavior from a pastor whose primary responsibility is to help people in trouble! And here he did not even have time to bother with an urgent case.

At that moment we knew that they really had no intention of paying what they owed us. We wanted to go back to Canada, but without that money we could not do it. Our furniture would have to remain in storage.

While I was awaiting in the church lobby, and my family stayed in the car, Mrs. Clemence Hinn—the mamma—accompanied by Willie Hinn's wife arrived in the OCC parking lot. The mother was preparing for her trip to Toronto.

Nicole and Melanie immediately walked towards her. Benny's mother knew us for we had met her the previous year at Christopher's house on Thanksgiving day. My wife told her everything: the promises, the way Benny mistreated us, our homeless situation. Mrs. Hinn was devastated, but not surprised.

With tears in her eyes she expressed her feelings, "I'm the mamma, and they don't care about me," adding, "Look what they've done to Christopher and Sammy. They pushed them out." And she strongly suggested, "Come to see Willie. Him he loves Jesus. He's not a businessman."

It was at this moment that we asked Mrs. Hinn if her dream of an infernal trio was true. The sweet lady did not say a word, but simply bowed her head as a sign of approval. We had our confirmation.

As per Mrs. Hinn's invitation, we went to the church of Willie on the following Sunday. When the service ended we explained to him the situation. He firmly recommended to go to the police. But we told him we had no signed contract. Then he said, "He asked for it. You did the job. Benny has to pay. You're not off-the-wall people."

We left the church and went to the first precinct on the road. We asked an officer about the legal recourses we had, but without a written contract, the only option we had was to consult a lawyer. This meant expenses we could not afford. We were really disappointed.

I had phoned the American immigration office in Miami several times to inquire about the green card lottery, but no trace of our names could be found. I called again and this time they gave me the confirmation that none of us had been selected.

That killed our hopes!

We had nothing else to do in Orlando.

We decided to sell the car. It had more than 90,000 miles on the odometer, and we could not afford paying the duty taxes on it to cross the border. A friend of ours that owned a used car lot bought the car. We got a fair price. That was a beginning.

However, the sum we received would not cover the costs of our transportation, lodging, food, and first few days in Canada. We also had to pay the monthly $75 for the storage unit, and eat while we spent our last days in Orlando.

We rented a motel room, because we were not to ask a member of OCC to offer us hospitality. They do not really appreciate you leaving the church of the "anointed" man. So we got a room where the price was most probably the cheapest. But it was not the safest.

We checked in, left our luggage, and went to storage to get some more. During our absence, someone utilizing the master key entered our room and stole two pieces of luggage that belonged to the children. The estimated value was $500, besides personal notes and papers that you simply cannot replace. We called the sheriff's department, and a police officer took down our statement. The motel manager felt sorry, but their insurance company would cover the losses.

I still had to find a way to get out of Orlando. All of a sudden I knew what to do and who to call. I grabbed the phone book, looked for the closest Canadian embassy, and called the one located in Miami.

I explained our situation for they had numerous questions. I told them the whole truth: the promises, the translation, the way Benny Hinn and members of his staff treated us. The lady told me that they could bring us back in Canada, but to the closest city—which would be Montreal. We had however the conviction to leave for Vancouver. She told me she would call back in a few days. We had nothing to worry about.

The Greyhound Bus lines held a special promotion for the summer season. You could travel to any place in the country for just sixty-eight dollars.

When the embassy lady called back she had good news. She had called OCC and wanted to talk to Benny but he was supposedly out of town. Instead, she talked with Gene Polino and asked him for our money. But on the account that there was no written contract, and despite the fact that Benny himself asked for the translation, Polino refused to pay our due.

The embassy official revealed that she had to shake and force him to pay our fares. As a result, Polino agreed that OCC would pay our bus fares. We could go to Seattle, Washington, then take a bus to Vancouver, Canada, for only twenty-two dollars extra.

She called back on Friday afternoon May 20. We were to leave Orlando the following Monday at one o'clock. To you dear lady, all the family want to express their gratitude.

Monday morning we took a cab, but we left without being reimbursed by the motel management. As previously agreed between the embassy and OCC, we went to the Salvation Army Center on Colonial Drive to pick up our bus tickets. The Center would then bring us to the bus depot. We found in that place love and compassion. People were so friendly and concerned. One sweet lady prepared a package for us containing all kinds of goodies, plus some money she had given out of her own pocket.

Leaving Orlando was for us an au revoir, not an adieu. Many questions remained unanswered. We were brokenhearted because the United States was home for us. We could not understand why we had to go through so many trials and tribulations.

We finally reached Seattle late Thursday night. Our bus for Vancouver would not leave until Friday at 9:30 A.M.

We arrived in Vancouver at two o'clock Friday afternoon, May 27, 1994. It was exactly two years after we left Montreal on May 27, 1992.

In spite of a strong conviction, we ignored at the time why we had moved to Vancouver. We rented a little apartment, then started to look for work in our respective fields and capacities.

I knew that faith healers were phony and dangerous people, and I knew they were not commissioned by God like they so pretend, but I had yet to discover with which power they operate. I then started researching the subject of faith healing. The city library of Vancouver is extremely well-equipped with books and literature on the subject. For a long time I had the desire to write a book to expose them. Through my research I unexpectedly discovered MESMERISM. This was the key.

Now I can assemble the puzzle of faith healing practices, and understand why Benny Hinn and others act the way they do every time and everywhere they utilize their "anointing."

Now we understand why we had felt a conviction to come to Vancouver. Now we can comprehend and accept the tribulations we suffered.

In Vancouver we were introduced by a pastor to a group of Christian leaders. One of them has especially caught my attention. While we were having lunch with him, although he did not do it purposely, that man revealed to us some priceless information. He said that he was a member of "The Gideons," a group of 300 hand-picked Christian leaders like David Cho, Benny Hinn, and many others. They believe they are chosen by God for a special purpose in these last days.

These 300 individuals reunite once a year to share, prepare and decide how to impact their own Christian spheres for the upcoming year. They are the unknown leaders of a fast growing and influential force. But why is it that they keep secret the existence of their group?

This explains why Benny Hinn would say, "The Lord has shown me to preach on this, and amazingly so and so has been preaching on the same subject. That's the work of the Holy Ghost!" These influential leaders are only following the direction taken by their secret group "The Gideons."

Please note that this group has no connection whatsoever with the Gideons International—those who distribute Bibles.

And since we were in Vancouver, we decided to check Henry Hinn, to visit his church. Benny had mentioned that more than 1,000 "first-class" people attended Henry's church. Upon our arrival we realized that the place contained approximately 300 chairs, and that the place was occupied at about fifty percent of its capacity. Benny had also declared that a revival would descend from Alaska. The "move of the Spirit" would pass by Vancouver, then continue further south on the west coast, than spread eastward to finally reach Orlando.

We were invited by a couple whom we had met in the apartment building where we lived. They really venerate Henry. The lady claims she was healed under his ministry. Since we knew Henry and his presumed "healing" ministry, we were really skeptical about her healing. She told us that, prior to her visit to Henry's church, she was confined to a wheelchair. Here is her story.

One Sunday night they went to his church. Henry walked in her direction, took her hands, and she rose up of her wheelchair—claiming to be completely healed. This lady has never been unable to walk, she only had problems to do so because of arthritis in her knees. This was confirmed to us by people who knew her. She was not confined to a wheelchair, she just felt more secure in it.

And from what I witnessed one night, she still has the same problem. Henry fooled her by placing her in a situation where she was the center of attention. Since he told her she was healed—even if it was not true—she now feels she has to live up to that image. We saw her slowly approaching the car in the underground garage of their residence. Not realizing that we could see her from the car, she acted naturally. She still limped!

Must I say that Henry's services are arranged just like his brother Benny's? The same songs, a similar church name. His church is named Vancouver Christian Center (quite similar to Orlando Christian Center)!

And Henry—just like his brother Benny—arrives on the platform after some praise and worship songs. When he spotted us, he became fearful. So during his preaching, he warned his flock against people that look religious and might come into the sanctuary, or just stand up during a service. That also, he said, justifies his use of bodyguards.

Henry also told the whole congregation that he would never forget the advice his brother Benny had given him. The advice was that people should always have money in their pockets when they go to church, "If you do not have money, then stay home."

After the service we proceeded to the front and gave him a sincere handshake. He mentioned that he was very busy, then said, "I don't know about your problems, and honestly I don't care about them." That confirmed what we thought of Henry Hinn—his answer reflected the state of his heart.

One day we saw him and his wife on Burrard Street in downtown Vancouver. We chatted with them but when we mentioned the name Alberto Carbone, Henry's wife grabbed his arm and they ran away from us. She probably felt we were stirring a stinking subject.

A short while later there was the Peter Popoff meeting, where I was hit by a "two-ton truck." We had been hurt emotionally, morally, financially; but it was the first time that a ministry would hurt us physically.

Now I really had to get to work and write a book exposing the True Face of the Fake Faith Healers.

AFTERWORD

> "I wouldn't have much to do with him, all the same!" said the Laird.
>
> "I'd sooner have any pain than have it cured in that unnatural way, and by such a man as that! He's a bad fellow, Svengali—I'm sure of it! He mesmerized you; that's what it is—mesmerism! I've often heard of it, but never seen it done before. They get you into their power, and just make you do any blessed thing they please— anything! and kill yourself into the bargain when they've done with you! It's just too terrible to think of!"
>
> George du Maurier in his novel *Trilby*

We were led to Orlando to discover and expose the true face of faith healers. Now we are glad that none of those guys hired us. If they had fulfilled their promises, we would have fallen into the same trap as so many others have.

If those faith healers are really sincere, if they dare to face the reality with a pure heart, this book will help them to see the damage they cause. This book will displease them because the knowledge of the truth impels changes. It is painful to change, and often unpleasing to receive rebukes. But rebukes are necessary.

Many good things came out of those ordeals. One of them is, I believe, that the people who will read the book, whoever they are, will realize that it is a jungle out there. This may shock but the truth is that in several Christian inner circles and back- stage of some huge ministries, the filthy discoveries found behind the scenes have nothing to envy to the rest of the world.

The source of the problem is that many of those men or women of God have let their ambitions and their human desires rule over their calling. They have changed God for mammon; changing their holiness for greediness.

I can declare today that we have not desired this role. We experienced times of plenty, times of famines; we wandered in valleys, and rejoiced on mountains. Through our adventures we were protected from several malicious snares by not getting fully involved with any of those guys.

I do not desire for my worst enemy to live what we have been through. We bear in our heart no trace of bitterness, no sign of hatred, or anger against any of the people we have known during those years, even though they have caused us great harm. On the contrary, I pray that one day the truth will set them free from their spiritual and financial bondage.

It is deplorable that the only way you can reach and touch those fake faith healers is if you expose them publicly with proof and evidence that will reveal their true face. Then they will react, then they will listen to what you have to say.

I also feel confident that this book will open the eyes of the spiritually blind, the eyes of the innocent people who sacrifice themselves almost to starvation to send money to such ministries. If those sweet people could only realize that they are not helping in building God's kingdom by sending their money to those preachers, but rather constructing the stepping stones in the erection of man's monuments. If we obtain such results, then all that we have suffered will not have been in vain.

Despite all the adventures we have lived through we have no regrets, no sorrows. Instead we have faith, hope, and love.

Our God is an awesome God.

If you have been hurt, mistreated, exploited by any ministry; or if you have questions or comments, please write to us at: Yves Brault c/o Dorrance Publishing 643 Smithfield Street Pittsburgh, PA 15222.

NOTES

CHAPTER ONE: SHEEP VS. WOLVES
1. This quote comes directly from the prayer request form handed out to us by Pastor Paul Collett on Monday, November 28, 1994, at Popoff's Miracle Service in Vancouver.

CHAPTER TWO: ON ROAD TO CALVARY
1. Jeremiah 28:9. All Scripture quotations used throughout this book are taken from the Holy Bible, New King James Version.

CHAPTER FOUR: THE ANOINT"HINN"G
1. Vincent Buranelli, *The Wizard from Vienna* (New York: Coward, McCann & Geoghegan, Inc., 1975), 115.
2. Ibid, 31.
3. James Wyckoff, *Franz Anton Mesmer: Between God and Devil*, (Englewood Cliffs: Prentice-Hall, Inc., 1975), 17.
4. Buranelli, *The Wizard from Vienna*, 116.
5. Ibid, 109. These comments are from Franz Anton Mesmer.
6. Ibid, 127.
7. Robert C. Fuller, *Mesmerism and the American Cure of Soul*, (Philadelphia: University of Pennsylvania Press, 1982), 72, citing the French mesmerist J.P.F. Deleuze's *Practical Instructions in Animal Magnetism*, 2d Ed. (New York: Samuel Wells, 1879). Its English translation served as one of the American mesmerists basic instruction manuals.
8. Wyckoff, *Franz Anton Mesmer: Between God and Devil*, 41.
9. Buranelli, *The Wizard from Vienna* 125.
10. Ibid, 132.
11. Fuller, *Mesmerism and the American Cure of Soul*, 6-7.
12. Buranelli, *The Wizard from Vienna*, 126.
13. Ibid, 126.
14. Wyckoff, *Franz Anton Mesmer: Between God and Devil*, 51.
15. Ibid, 53.
16. Buranelli, *The Wizard from Vienna*, 115.
17. Fuller, *Mesmerism and the American Cure of Soul*, 125.
18. Buranelli, *The Wizard from Vienna*, 152.
19. Wyckoff, *Franz Anton Mesmer: Between God and Devil*, 47.
20. Buranelli, *The Wizard from Vienna*, 67-68.
21. Ibid, 125.
22. Fuller, *Mesmerism and the American Cure of Soul*, 3.

23. Wyckoff, *Franz Anton Mesmer: Between God and Devil*, 54.
24. Ibid, 55.
25. Buranelli, *The Wizard from Vienna*, 110. Extract of the royal commission report.
26. Wyckoff, *Franz Anton Mesmer: Between God and Devil*, 86, citing Margaret Goldsmith, *Franz Anton Mesmer—A History of Mesmerism* (New York: Doubleday, Doran, 1934), 134-135.

CHAPTER SIX: THE ACADEMY AWARDS: THE JUDAS

1. Fuller, *Mesmerism and the American Cure of Soul*, 78, citing Whitney R. Cross, *The Burned-Over District*. (Ithaca: Cornell University Press, 1950), 183.
2. Fuller, *Mesmerism and the American Cure of Soul*, 78.
3. Jamie Buckingham, *Daughter of Destiny*, (Plainfield: Logos International, 1976), 139.
4. Ibid, 143.
5. Ibid, 144.
6. Ibid, 153.
7. Ibid, 203.
8. Ibid, 220.
9. Ibid, 221.
10. Ibid, 221.
11. Ibid, 248.
12. Hank Hanegraaff, *Christianity in Crisis*, (Eugene: Harvest House Publishers, 1993), 340-341.
13 Ibid., 341. Cf. Preston, M.D., medical analysis report, 28 October 1992; CRI telephone interviews with Dr. Preston Simpson, 6 and 23 October 1992, emphasis in the original.
14. Hank Hanegraaff, "A Summary Critique: Lord, I Need a Miracle," *Christian Research Journal Reprint*, 1-2. This article originally appeared in the Summer 1993 *Christian Research Journal*.
15. Wyckoff, *Franz Anton Mesmer: Between God and Devil*, 60.
16. Hanegraaff, *Christianity in Crisis*, 341, citing Benny Hinn, "Double Portion Anointing, Part #3 (Orlando, FL: Orlando Christian Center, n.d.), audiotape A031791-3, sides 1-2; aired on TBN, 7 April 1991.
17. Benny Hinn interviewed by Stephen Strang, "Q & A Benny Hinn Speaks Out" — *Charisma*, August 1993, 25-26.
18. Anthony Quinn with Daniel Paisner, *One Man Tango*, (New York: Harper Collins Publishers, 1995), 66.
19. Ibid, 67.
20. James Morris, *The Preachers*, (New York: St. Martin's Press, 1973), 57.
21. Larry Martz with Ginny Carroll, *Ministry of Greed*, (New York: Weidenfeld & Nicolson, 1988), 14.
22. Ibid, 14, 12.
23. Michael Richardson, *The Edge of Disaster*, (New York: St. Martin's Press, 1987), 29.
24. Ibid, 116.

25. Ibid, 125.
26. Joe E. Barnhart, *Jim and Tammy*, (New York: Prometheus Books, 1988), 67.
27. Warren W. Wiersbe, *The Essential Everyday Bible Commentary*, (Nashville: Thomas Nelson Publishers, 1993), 1202.
28. Richardson, *The Edge of Disaster*, 130.
29. Ibid, 132.
30. Ibid, 133.
31. Ibid, 138.
32. Ibid, 139.
33. Ibid, 151-152.
34. Ibid, 152-153. Emphasis in the original.
35. Ibid, 186-189.
36. Ibid, 191.
37. Ibid, 200.
38. Ibid, 211.
39. Interview of the reporter Tony Pipitone with Benny Hinn, WCPX-TV Channel 6 NEWS, 3 March 1993.
40. Larry Martz with Ginny Carroll, *Ministry of Greed*, (New York: Weidenfeld & Nicolson, 1988), 12.
41. Richardson, *The Edge of Disaster*, 72.
42. Wiersbe, *The Essential Everyday Bible Commentary*, 1419.

CHAPTER SEVEN: IT'S A SIN TO TELL A LIE
1. Deuteronomy 18:21-22, Jeremiah 28:9.
2. Fuller, *Mesmerism and the American Cure of Soul*, 19-20.

CHAPTER NINE: ON ROAD TO SINGAPORE
1. James Morris, *The Preachers*, (New York: St. Martin's Press, 1973), 21.
2. *Official Hotel Guide*, (Secaucus: Reed Travel Group, 1993). Description of all the hotels of the world can be found in the *Official Hotel Guide*, published annually by Reed Travel Group.
3. Gary Tidwell, *Anatomy of a Fraud*, (New York: John Wiley & Sons, Inc., 1993), 286.

CHAPTER TEN: A VALLEY OF TEARS
1. Roberts Liardon, *I Saw Heaven*, (Tulsa: Harrison House, 1983), 19.
2. Ibid, 26.
3. Wiersbe, The Essential Everyday Bible Commentary, 748. Thomas Carlyle is the author of the quote.

CHAPTER ELEVEN: "HINN"SIDE EDITION: BENNY "HINN"SIDE OUT
1. Steve Wilson and Charles Dalaklis, *Inside Edition*, Benny Hinn shouting on stage while he is standing behind several wheelchairs (2 March 1993).
2. Mary Hamill, WCPX-TV *Channel 6 NEWS*, (3 March 1993).
3. Steve Wilson and Charles Dalaklis, *Inside Edition*, the lady lays on the floor, the

crowd thinks that something great is happening to her. Benny has successfully spread the belief that people fall down because he has an "anointing" (2 March 1993).

4. Ibid. Three weeks later Benny was running this "miracle" on his TV program.
5. Ibid.
6. Ibid.
7. Mary Hamill, WCPX-TV *Channel 6 NEWS*, (3 March 1993).
8. Fuller, *Mesmerism and the American Cure of Soul*, 125.
9. Benny Hinn, *Praise the Lord* program on TBN, aired live 4 March, 1993.
10. Hinn interviewed by Tony Pipitone, WCPX-TV *Channel 6 NEWS*, (2 March 1993).
11. Ibid.
12. Hinn on *Praise the Lord*, (4 March 1993).
13. Host Paul Crouch on *Praise the Lord*, (4 March 1993). Paul's admiration for a man like Benny Hinn makes you really wonder if he has not already kept company too long with the wrong crowd.
14. "Schweiz: Kritik af Benny Hinn" (Switzerland: Criticism of Benny Hinn). *Udfordringen*, 15 September 1994, Side 2. Translated from Danish by Suresh Jeyasingham.
15. Hinn interviewed by Tony Pipitone, WCPX-TV *Channel 6 NEWS*, (3 March 1993).
16. Hinn on *Praise the Lord*, (4 March 1993).
17. Ibid. It is one of Benny's strongest points to say something to one crowd, and something different to another; whatever is more advantageous to him, he says.
18. Hinn interviewed by Stephen Strang, "Q & A Benny Hinn Speaks Out," Charisma, August 1993, 26.
19. Hinn on *Praise the Lord*, (4 March 1993).
20. Hinn interviewed by Strang, Charisma, 26.
21. Hinn on *Praise the Lord*, (4 March 1993).
22. Ibid. It is a real problem that his personal secretary intentionally hides letters and incoming calls from him. She did it with us, she did it with *Inside Edition*; how many more?
23. Ibid.
24. Hinn interviewed by Bill O'Reilly, *Inside Edition*, (26 March 1993).

CHAPTER TWELVE: OH! HENRY

1. James Morris, *The Preachers*, (New York: St. Martin's Press, 1973), 1. A.A. Allen's message to Brother Marjoe.

CHAPTER FOURTEEN: HANGING TO AN AIR MATTRESS ON A RAGING SEA

1. Christopher Hitchens, "No Saint," *The Weekend Sun*, 26 November 1994, 1(B).
2. Buranelli, *The Wizard from Vienna*, 116-117.
3. G. Richard Fisher and M. Kurt Goedelman, "A Summary Critique: Welcome, Holy Spirit," *Christian Research Journal*, Winter 1996, 49-50.
4. Ibid.
5. Hinn on his program *This is Your Day*, heard on June 6 and 8, 1995, on KNTR Ferndale, WA.